GEORGE SCHARF'S LONDON

GEORGE SCHARF'S LONDON

*Sketches and Watercolours
of a Changing City, 1820-50*

PETER JACKSON

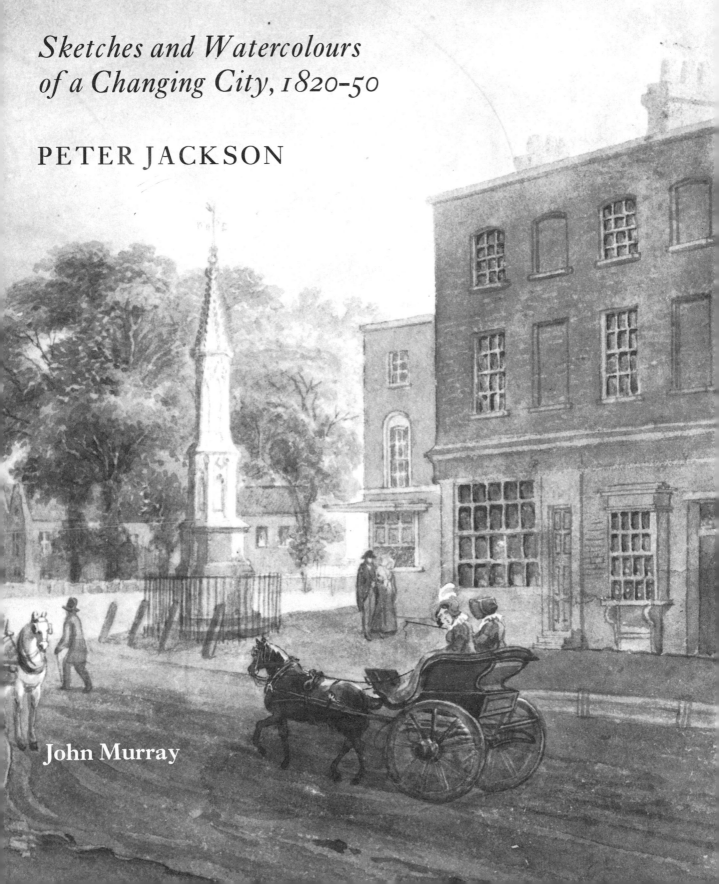

John Murray

Text © Peter Jackson 1987

Illustration material of which the original is held by the
British Museum © Trustees of the British Museum 1987

First published 1987
by John Murray (Publishers) Ltd
50 Albemarle Street, London WIX 4BD

Printed in Great Britain by
BAS Printers Limited, Over Wallop, Hampshire

British Library Cataloguing in Publication Data
Scharf, George
    George Scharf's London: sketches and
    watercolours of a changing city, 1820–50.
    1. Scharf, George   2. London (England)
    in art
    I. Title   II. Jackson, Peter
    709.2′4   N6767.S/

    ISBN 0–7195–4379–7

TITLE-PAGE: TOTTENHAM, 1822

*The High Cross still stands at this busy road
junction in Tottenham High Road looking exactly
as George Scharf has drawn it. The original cross
went back to the Middle Ages but about 1600 it was
rebuilt in brick and in 1809 it was encased in cement
and given its gothic appearance. The Swan tavern,
where Izaac Walton is reputed to have stayed when
he came here to fish, still stands but is altered out
of all recognition*

CONTENTS

Acknowledgements

My thanks must go, first, to Iain Bain of the Tate Gallery who suggested that I should
do a book about George Scharf. Support over a long period came from Antony Wood and
once John Murray had undertaken publication I received the most enthusiastic encouragement from John R. Murray himself and everyone at 50 Albemarle Street especially my
editor, Duncan McAra, and the designer Joe Whitlock Blundell.

I am grateful to Fred Schwarzbach of Washington University who introduced me to
George Scharf's notebooks and to Valerie Vaughan of the National Portrait Gallery,
London, for her patience in allowing a slow reader plenty of time to make notes from them.
To her I am also indebted for help in obtaining Scharf's portrait.

Without the co-operation of Mr A. V. Griffiths, Deputy Keeper of the Department of
Prints & Drawings at the British Museum, this book would not have been possible and
I must thank everyone who works in his department for their ever-ready assistance and
for their prompt and tireless delivery of the weighty volumes in which the Scharf drawings
are mounted.

The British Museum photography was undertaken by Graham Javes who produced the
most wonderful results from what was sometimes very difficult material. At the British
Museum, also, I would like to thank Janet Wallace, Archivist, for information about the
Scharf bequests.

Ralph Hyde at the Guildhall has, as usual, been an unfailing source of help and encouragement; so, too, has David Webb of Bishopsgate Institute. I must thank John Phillips, Curator
at the Greater London Record Office, for finding some interesting early drawings by George
Scharf jun.; Jean Pegram, of Haringey Library, for her considerable local knowledge; and
Julian Watson, of Woodlands Library, who helped me so much with Woolwich.

Finally, I wish to thank Yale Center for British Art, Paul Mellon Collection, for their
generous permission to reproduce the watercolour on page 103.

P.J.

George Scharf's Workaday London

The work of George Scharf has never been widely known and his name appears only rarely in histories of art. The reason for this is not difficult to understand. The bulk of his prodigious output was unknown to the general public of his own day and even now can be seen only in the British Museum and a few local collections. He earned his livelihood by producing drawings for scientific bodies and learned journals, painstaking and meticulous work valued by scholars but unknown outside their circle.

He was not a book illustrator and his printed works, though of very high standard, were far from numerous and published as individual prints, hand-coloured and expensive. But, above all, his paintings were not to the public's taste and although he exhibited twenty-eight pictures at the Royal Academy, four at the Suffolk Street Gallery and fourteen at the New Water Colour Society, he never once, during forty years, sold a single picture.

There were some highly competent topographical artists who were content to work in the commercial field, most notably Thomas Hosmer Shepherd, Scharf's contemporary, who never exhibited at the Royal Academy but who produced 350 drawings to illustrate Elme's *Metropolitan Improvements: London in the Nineteenth Century*. But these views, accurate and charming as they are, show buildings either brand-new or long-famous. We look in vain for the little lanes and alleys, the market sheds, the coffee-houses and shops. For these we turn to George Scharf who delighted in sketching such things. He shows us the more down-to-earth workaday London shortly before photography and pictorial journalism made such scenes commonplace. He derived particular satisfaction from sketching the demolition or the erection of buildings and was fascinated by the details of scaffolding and machinery involved. For this he could not have been working at a more opportune time.

London in the decade before Victoria came to the throne and during the early part of her reign was in a state of flux. When Scharf arrived in England in 1816, London was about to shake off the architectural lethargy created by the economic demands of the Napoleonic wars and John Nash was busy with his grandiose plans for creating a Regency London of classical stucco. London was changing its character completely. Whole areas were being demolished to make way for improvements. Regent Street cut right through the slums of Soho; Trafalgar Square was being created out of the squalor of Charing Cross; and a shining new Covent Garden Market was rising from a clutter of ancient stalls. The approaches to New London Bridge were sweeping away huge sections of the City and Southwark, and whole districts were being transformed by the inexorable march of the railway. London was being tidied up. The widening of thoroughfares meant the wholesale destruction of hundreds of those little bow-windowed shops so typical of the eighteenth century and Scharf hastened to make a record of them before they were swept away for ever. It is our good fortune that he was at hand to record in his sketchbooks building activity great and small from the construction of the British Museum and the Houses of Parliament to the erection of Marble Arch and the new corner shop.

But it is for his observations of London life that we must be most grateful. Sketchbook after sketchbook was filled with drawings of the ordinary people of London going about their everyday business. Street hawkers and musicians, vendors of hot potatoes and lemonade, beggars and milk-maids, dustmen with their carts, draymen with their wagons, Punch-and-Judy shows and performing animals, all the teeming life of early Victorian London is here in his pages.

He used some of his studies of workmen in his published lithographs, particularly those of London Bridge, and he may have intended to use some sketches as preliminary notes for later work. Indeed, there is every reason to believe that he wanted to do a series of views of the shops in the Strand based on his numerous drawings but was unable to find a publisher who was interested. However, the vast majority of these hundreds of sketches were purely for his own enjoyment and relaxation. He found his bread-and-butter work tiresome and boring. This becomes very clear from his notebooks where he carefully records every minute spent on the laborious task of stippling texture on a lithographic stone to render with minute accuracy the shading on fossils and bones sometimes life-size and enormous. A more soul-destroying task for an artist is difficult to imagine. Little wonder that he welcomed the freedom of sketching in the street; it was his hobby and he delighted in it.

The bulk of George Scharf's work, which includes finished watercolours in addition to sketches and pencil drawings, was sold by his widow to the British Museum in 1862; others were given by his son George in 1900. They remained bundled up in parcels for years and even today, in the official catalogue of Drawings of the British School, they are listed as packets containing dozens and even hundreds of drawings. One packet contained no fewer than 358 drawings. They have now been sorted out and mounted in six large albums and five solander cases. There is also a substantial number of drawings, including his German ones, in the Department of Manuscripts of the British Library. The Guildhall also holds some interesting material particularly the work Scharf did for the City Corporation, but not all his drawings are in the British Museum and the Guildhall.

There are a number of drawings in private hands and scattered throughout London's local collections. But a curious fact emerges upon examination of this material. Several drawings are duplicates of ones in the British Museum. They are not just different versions of the same view but exact copies even to the inclusion of pencil notes and bearing the same dates. It would seem that these were copies he made for friends and that they were later acquired by John Edmund Gardner whose great London collection was auctioned at Sotheby's in 1923. There were certainly Scharf drawings in the sale as he is mentioned by name in the catalogue. Some may have been given to Gardner by George Scharf jun. who knew him well and did some drawings of his own for his collection.

Scharf taught both his sons to draw as indeed he taught his wife Elizabeth. In 1825, on one of his rare breaks from work, he took her to Woolwich and they each did a drawing of the same cottage. Young Henry combined his limited drawing ability with his love of the theatre and in the Enthoven Collection at the Victoria and Albert Museum are several pencil drawings of the scenery at Covent Garden which he sketched when he was seventeen years old.

George jun. showed the greater artistic ability, however, and was his father's favourite. Their birthdays were so close together, separated by only eight days, that poor Henry, who was born on 8 December, had to wait until 16 December to share his birthday with his brother.

They were totally different characters. George grew up to be a rather pompous establishment figure who virtually founded the National Portrait Gallery and was knighted for his work. He gives the impression of being rather ashamed of his father for no apparent reason. Henry, on the other hand, was a happy-go-lucky Bohemian who adored his father and tried in vain to please him in academic work for which he was not suited. Finally he gave up trying and went on the stage where he was quite successful especially in America.

George Scharf's life was uneventful. Virtually all we know of it is recorded in his journals and notebooks, now in the National Portrait Gallery. They make dull reading. They are a diary of unremitting work, a meticulous record of hours spent on commissions and his carefully worked-out charges. He never appears to have taken a holiday apart from the odd brief excursion down the Thames and back. Discounting his trip to Bavaria for family reasons, he never seems to have strayed farther from London than Herne Bay. His only amusement was to take the boys to the Zoo or to see a railway being built and, later, the occasional visit to the theatre, but then only to see Henry on the stage. He indulged in no extravagances and spent what little he earned in keeping a comfortable household and giving his sons a good education.

Towards the end of his life he was desperately short of money, and he would have died alone and in poverty had not illness overcome his stubborn independence and forced him to accept his son George's grudging charity. He died intestate but the legacy he left in his drawings is of inestimable value to us now and it is to be hoped that the appearance at last of a selection of his work, much of it never before published, will accord him the recognition he has been denied for so long.

GEORGE SCHARF

George Scharf was born in the small town of Mainburg in Bavaria on 23 April 1788, the son of Andreas and Franziska Scharf. At the age of thirteen he left home to live in Geisenfeld, a village about ten miles from his home town where, in 1802, he began taking drawing lessons from Herr Kiermayer a painter of religious subjects, and three years later he secured a place in the Royal Academy of Arts and Sciences in Munich. While there he was able to benefit from the study of the splendid collection of Old Masters at the Pinakothek, Munich's famous art gallery, which he copied diligently. On one occasion he was noticed by King Maximilian of Bavaria who bought his copy of a portrait of Prince Eugene Beauharnis.

But most importantly Munich was the birthplace of lithography and Scharf was able to study the infant art and get caught up in the enthusiasm for the new-found medium. Alois Senefelder had invented the new printing process only a few years previously and Scharf's tutor, Professor Joseph Hauber, was one of lithography's earliest exponents and a contributor to a book called *Lithographische Kunstprodukte* which was the first important collection of lithographs to be published in Germany.

By the time he left the Royal Academy of Munich in 1810 Scharf was not only an expert in the technicalities of lithography but an accomplished miniature portraitist and he began to earn his living by wandering through France and the Low Countries seeking commissions. With Europe in a ferment of military activity resulting from the Napoleonic wars there was no shortage of sitters – officers and men of both armies were only too pleased to be portrayed in their magnificent uniforms.

We can trace his wanderings at this time from his dated drawings and sketchbooks. In 1811 he was in Verdun, in 1812 in Cambrai, and in 1813 he was with the Prussian army at Mechlin. It was while at the small Belgian town of Mechlin that his life was to take a new direction. The Prussians suddenly received orders to march to Antwerp to hinder the French general Carnot and Scharf was advised to make his way to the British headquarters at Calmpthout. As a result Scharf joined the British army as a 'lieutenant of baggage' in the Engineers and saw action at the Battle of Waterloo. After Waterloo he accompanied the allied armies to Paris where he made numerous sketches of the camp in the Bois de Boulogne.

Attracted, presumably, by the descriptions of London he must have heard from his British comrades, Scharf left Paris on New Year's Day 1816 and on 5 January he landed at Dover. Here he immediately painted the castle standing on the white cliffs before setting out for London where he was to spend the rest of his life.

The first painting he ever did in London was a watercolour, *Islington from the New River*, but he obviously intended to earn his living as a portrait painter and in 1816 he did a self-portrait miniature to show to prospective clients as an example of his skill. (A photograph of this painting is in the National Portrait Gallery but its present whereabouts is not known.) The following year he was able to send seven portraits to the Royal Academy and he also painted the political radicals Thistlewood, Watson, Preston and Hooper while they were on trial. The paintings were later copied as a stipple engraving entitled *The Spa Fields Rioters* although he did not actually engrave the plate.

At this time an event occurred which was to have a profound influence on his future work. On 10 June 1818 Parliament was dissolved and electioneering began. To George Scharf, living at the time in St Martin's Lane, it must have seemed that the entire population of London was gathering almost on his doorstep as the electors of Westminster converged on Covent Garden day after day for nearly three weeks to hear their Parliamentary candidates addressing them from the hustings. It was a marvellous opportunity to observe the Londoner in holiday mood and it is possibly this carnival event that sparked off Scharf's lifelong fascination for the ordinary people of workaday London.

1 George Scharf, aged about twenty-eight. This self-portrait is probably the miniature he painted on his arrival in England as an example of his work to show prospective clients; from a photograph in the National Portrait Gallery, London, of the original miniature, the present whereabouts of which is unknown

Based on dozens of sketches, he made a watercolour drawing showing the bustling scene in Covent Garden and set about getting it published as a print. He found a sponsor in Colnaghi's, the print sellers of Cockspur Street and in November 1818 it was produced as an aquatint[1]. Two years later there was a new general election and Scharf republished his old print merely altering the date and a few names. But he had no interest in who was being elected; the picture was merely an excuse for drawing a crowd of Londoners going about their business. So fascinated was he by these foreground figures that he produced a small key plate to accompany the print showing in simple etched line some of the principal market characters and identifying in French and German their trades and occupations. It was a fascination which was never to leave him and for the rest of his life he would carry a sketchbook in which to jot down the everyday people of London's streets.

He never let an opportunity for sketching pass by and his journals are full of occasions when he has made use of the idle moment. He records calling on the Earl of Derby on some business, couldn't see him but sketched his dining room, and while attending an inquest in his local pub he 'made a sketch of the jury assembled'. He hated being idle. 'Sketched from the coach while horses were changing on the Cambridge Road' he scribbled on the back of a rough drawing of some unidentified buildings.

George Scharf's first London address was No 3 St Martin's Lane which was a shop with two floors of living accommodation above reached by a side door. The property was owned by Mary Hicks who ran the business of Grocer and Cheesemonger and lived above the shop with her younger sister Elizabeth[2]. For a time the shop was rented to John Cannan, Oilman, but the rooms above continued to be occupied by the Hicks sisters and

2 Coronation Procession of His Majesty King George IV, 19 July 1821: Scharf's lithograph published on 20 August 1821. The processional route was actually covered with an awning; Scharf has dispensed with it for a better view

3 St Paul's, Shadwell: a plate from the *Gentleman's Magazine*, March 1823

George Scharf who had his own nameplate under a bell-pull by the side of the door. Elizabeth Hicks was little more than two years older than George Scharf and, not surprisingly, a close relationship developed between them. They were married at the church of St Martin-in-the-Fields on 20 August 1820[3] and their son George was born four months later on 16 December 1820. Their second son, Henry, was born on 8 December 1822.

With the responsibility of a family to support, Scharf now turned his hand to any artistic work which came his way. He abandoned the idea of earning his living as a portrait painter and became, what we would call today, a commercial artist. His experience in lithography now proved to be invaluable. Lithography, which had fallen into the doldrums since its introduction into England in about 1801, was now being actively promoted by such printers as Rudolph Ackermann, Charles Joseph Hullmandel and Francis Moser. Scharf, as one of the few artists in London with any knowledge of the medium, found himself in demand.

One of his earliest commissions was a view of the Coronation Procession of George IV in 1821 which he lithographed for Thomas Clay the printseller at 18 Ludgate Hill. It was printed by Charles Hullmandel, the most influential lithographic printer of his day. Hullmandel, one year younger than Scharf and with a similar German background, befriended the artist and even recommended him for all sorts of odd jobs; one was to draw a vase and a tray for the silversmiths Wiltshire & Son of 36 Cornhill presumably for use on their billheads and advertising literature. And possibly on the recommendation of Hullmandel who printed it, Scharf lithographed a view of the church of St Paul's, Shadwell, for the March 1823 issue of the *Gentleman's Magazine*. He also dabbled in book illustration. In 1822 he worked on John Parton's *Some Account of the Hospital and Parish of St Giles-in-*

B. Howlet fecit 1817.   G. Scharf Lithog.

Houses, Great Queen Street.

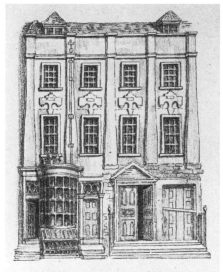

Entrance to Queen St Chapel.

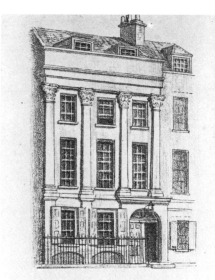

House formerly of Sir Rob. Strange

the-Fields producing thirteen lithographs of buildings, some drawn directly on the site and some merely copies of drawings done by others years before.

But these odd jobs were not enough to support a growing family particularly as Scharf always underpriced his work and hated asking for money[4]. He sought more regular employment and found it in illustrating scientific works and the journals of learned societies. The Royal College of Surgeons and the Geological Society employed him and he numbered among his clients scientists as eminent as Charles Darwin and Sir Richard Owen. Minutely detailed lithographs of bones and fossils, geological strata and scientific specimens of all sorts were to be his principal source of income for the rest of his life.

His journals and notebooks show him to be an indefatigably hard worker who began at 5 or 6 a.m. and frequently spent ten hours working solidly. He valued his time at two shillings an hour which, in theory, should have brought him in a reasonable income but he frequently reduced the total sum by pounds and even then was not paid the full amount he asked for.

He was hopeless at business. Hullmandel in a letter telling him about a small job he had recommended him to do wrote, 'I know your prices are very moderate – often too much so, I therefor think it better to let you know that you may ask a price which may pay you as they expect it will come high.'

There was no shortage of work in those early days. His skill and reliability were in great demand and it was work for which his painstaking accuracy well qualified him. But there was little artistic satisfaction in the work and he found the laborious discipline it imposed very tedious. He sought relaxation in sketching his street characters and took a special delight in drawing scenes of demolition.

He found ample opportunity for this indulgence in 1830 when that part of St Martin's Lane in which he was living was pulled down to make way

4 Illustrations comprising a plate from John Parton's *Some Account of the Hospital and Parish of St Giles-in-the-Fields* to which Scharf contributed thirteen lithographs in 1822

5 The back yard of George Scharf's house, No 14 Francis Street, with its outside toilet, rainwater barrel and coal bunker. The house two doors away is under repair. This view was drawn in 1844

6 The kitchen in George Scharf's house, No 14 Francis Street. This highly detailed watercolour was painted 'from recollection whilst at Munich in 1846', according to a note Scharf later added to a pencil sketch he had made three years before

7 (*opposite*) The Lord Mayor's Dinner, 9 November 1828: Scharf's retouched proof for the lithograph published on 1 October 1829

for Trafalgar Square. Scharf celebrated his departure from his old lodgings with a drawing of its demolition and nailed a notice on the door announcing that he had moved to 14 Francis Street. He took with him his sister-in-law, Mary Hicks, 'a second mother to the boys' as he once referred to her. Francis Street[5], a turning off the east side of Tottenham Court Road, had been built in 1772 and No 14 must have been a charming residence with a view from its back windows of an early eighteenth-century farmhouse[6] and a tree-lined 'ride' leading to it from Tottenham Court Road.

Throughout 1830 New London Bridge was being constructed and the demolition of whole streets to make the approach roads was an irresistible subject for George Scharf's pencil.

Two years before, he had painted the Guildhall banquet and published it as a lithograph dedicated to the Lord Mayor, the Sheriffs and Common Council. Obviously impressed by his work the London Bridge Committee now commissioned him to record the building of the new bridge. They could not have made a better choice. Scharf made the most of his opportunity and produced what is undoubtedly his finest work. Based on scores of drawings representing hundreds of hours sketching on the site he produced two watercolour paintings, each 5 ft long. They must have been remarkably impressive. Sadly we will now never know for they were both destroyed when the Guildhall Art Gallery was bombed in 1941. Fortunately Scharf made lithographs of them which show his wonderful draughtsmanship and attention to detail. The work took him far longer and was more difficult than he had anticipated and he wrote a letter to the Bridge Committee on 19 July 1830 explaining his slowness in producing the lithographs which had to be made on four stones, two for each of the 5 ft long paintings. His original estimate for the work was £20 for each painting and £30 for

each lithograph. This he now realised was too low and he expressed a hope that the Committee would grant him some extra payment.

In 1835 Scharf offered three drawings to the London Bridge Committee which had been commissioned originally by Sir John Rennie, architect of the new bridge. Scharf had taken such a long time in producing them that when they finally arrived Rennie denied that he had ordered them. One was of Crooked Lane with St Michael's Church which he had exhibited at the Royal Academy in 1832; the other two were of Old and New London Bridge from Thames Street and from Southwark. The Committee agreed to purchase them at a sum not exceeding £30. There followed some extra-ordinary bargaining. Scharf wrote in his journal for 27 January 1835: 'Called on Mr Jones[7], Chairman of the London Bridge Committe, who told me that the Committee offer me £25 instead of £33 for the three draw-ings upon which I said I must have £30. He mentioned then £27 10s. Still I stood out for thirty which he said he would endeavour to get me if he could.' Scharf received his £30 but Jones got his revenge for having failed to beat him down by refusing him permission to borrow one of his paintings for an exhibition.

The same year that the Scharf family went to live in Francis Street University College School was founded and, as it was only round the corner in Gower Street, young George and Henry Scharf were numbered among its first scholars[8]. In August 1833 Scharf produced his lively lithograph of the school. He proudly presented some proofs to the Master who was

8 Scharf's lithograph of University College School playground: the school was opened in 1830 as an adjunct to University College, the large domed building on the left, known at this time as the University of London. It was founded in 1826 to provide university education for non-Anglicans excluded from Oxford and Cambridge

no doubt a little taken aback when Scharf arrived at the annual prize-giving carrying sixty-five copies of the print, twenty of which he sold on the spot.

On 16 October 1834 the Houses of Parliament caught fire and burnt all through the night. The next morning Scharf was on the spot clambering over the smouldering ruins busy with his sketchbook. Some days later when the ruins became dangerous he went up on the lead roof of Westminster Hall, which had miraculously escaped the fire, and began to sketch a panoramic view. He became so engrossed that he worked until darkness fell when he found that the door through which he had come had been locked. Shouts for help resulted in his rescue over some roofs, down a ladder, and through the house of the Yeoman Usher of the Exchequer, William Godwin. Mrs Godwin was highly amused with the adventure. She told Scharf that he could go through her house any time he wanted to.

He certainly took full advantage of her offer. Almost every day for three weeks he went through her house to go sketching on the roof of Westminster Hall, and on at least one occasion he took his wife Elizabeth and a party of friends with him to see the view. The boys accompanied him sometimes and George jun. produced his own watercolour of the scene.[9] Scharf must have felt indebted to Mrs Godwin for all the inconvenience he had caused her and when she asked him to do some drawings of Herne Bay for her he readily agreed.

Scharf's view of the ruins of the Houses of Parliament was a huge watercolour about 10 ft long by 2 ft 6 in. high painted in halves and joined together which he finished on 30 March 1835 just in time for the New Water Colour Society's annual exhibition at Exeter Hall in the Strand.

It received favourable notices in the papers. The art critic of the *Atlas* wrote: 'The most remarkable drawing is that of Mr Scharf (No 160) which is of enormous size, and represents with great fidelity, and in a powerful and spirited manner, the ruins at Westminster, while the fire was yet unsubdued and smouldering on the floors and the workmen were already busy on the walls – here taking down, there building up. The scene, in all its bearings, is perfect.'

Scharf was very proud of this great work and decided to publish it as a print. To advertise the project he produced a prospectus showing a small sketch of the picture and outlining his plan: 'A lithographic print to be published of the above half the size of the original which is about 10 ft long and the print to be 4 ft 8 in. by 1 ft 6 in. on two sheets imperial. Price £1 plain, £2 coloured. Names of subscribers are received in the Exhibition Room by the Artist.'[10]

Scharf obviously had great hopes for this project but it came to nothing. Only one person promised to subscribe while the painting was on exhibition in Exeter Hall, but he received another ten names when he was permitted to hang it in the Committee Room of the House of Lords. Among the potential subscribers here were the Duke of Wellington and Charles Barry, the architect of the new Houses of Parliament.

9 Printed prospectus for the *Panoramic View of the Ruins of the late Houses of Parliament* in the Guildhall Library. Its puzzling perspective begins to make some sense only if the two ends are joined to form a circle in which the viewer stands with Westminster Abbey behind him/her

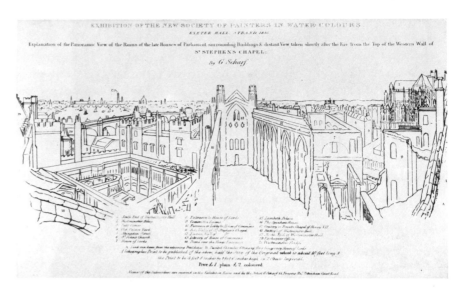

However, although Scharf continued to exhibit the painting for years all over London, he failed to find enough subscribers to make the project worth while and we must assume that he abandoned the idea for no trace of this lithograph has ever come to light. As for the original painting, Scharf clearly had a great fondness for it and exhibited it on any occasion which presented itself, carrying it from gallery to gallery and fussing over its hanging. Its end was sad. A few months before he died Scharf, desperately short of money, was obliged to put it up for auction and one of the last entries in his journal reads: 'My two large pictures of the Ruins of the Houses of Parliament I sent to Messrs Christy's [*sic*] Sale Room and only got £2 10s for them to a Mr Palmer of No 12 St James's Place.'[11]

For years Scharf had been doing scientific drawings for the Zoological Society and after they opened their gardens in Regent's Park he was able to publish on his own account a beautiful set of views which he was allowed to sell at the entrance gates. The Zoo's first giraffes arrived in the gardens on 25 May 1836 and two days later Scharf was there with young George to draw them and the Arab keepers who accompanied them. While he was at work Queen Adelaide arrived to see the giraffes, was very impressed with Scharf's drawing, and asked for all his zoological views. Three weeks later Scharf published his lithograph of the giraffes and took it to Buckingham Palace. He did not see the Queen again but the print was shown to her and she ordered three coloured copies together with three sets of the Zoo views.

The giraffes were Scharf's bestseller. On 24 June he wrote that they sold so well 'that I could not get them ready fast enough, sold 500 in two weeks'. And towards the end of the year he was commissioned by John Ridgeway, the Staffordshire Potter, to design a jug decorated with his giraffes modelled in relief. As payment Ridgeway offered him a tea or dinner

service but Scharf wanted cash. For in spite of the success of his Zoo prints his profit for the whole year 1836 was only £50. The financial troubles which were to beset him for the rest of his life were just beginning.

He resigned from the New Water Colour Society 'in consequence of my being unable to continue paying the subscription of six shillings a month' and he took Henry away from London University School and set him to study anatomical drawing with Professor Owen at the College of Surgeons. George jun. had already left school and was working at the British Museum drawing antique sculpture. But neither of the boys was bringing in any money yet and their father had to find additional means of employment. He began to give drawing lessons and even did work for a toy manufacturer lithographing figures 'which were to be cut out of card for a Si-Saw'. He tried to persuade Charles Knight, the publisher of the very popular *Penny Magazine*, to use his drawings of the Strand without success, but he received more encouraging news at the end of 1837.

He had sent a set of his views of the Zoological Gardens to the Queen of Bavaria and now the Bavarian Ambassador, Baron Cetto, sent for him and on behalf of the Queen paid him 100 florins or over £9, 'which', wrote Scharf, 'showed a comparatively poor Bavarian Queen so much more

10 London Zoo's first giraffes, lithographed by Scharf in 1836; with them are their three native attendants and, on the right, M. Thibout, a French trader in the Sudan who had been commissioned, for a fee of £700, to find giraffes for the Zoological Society. The animals caused a sensation when they walked through the streets from Blackwall where they landed.

liberal, as the rich Queen of England only gave 14 shillings for the same prints'.

Meanwhile Scharf was continuing his scientific work at the Geological Society for Charles Darwin who was collating and describing the specimens he had brought back with him from his voyage in the *Beagle*. One of these specimens was part of the skull of Toxodon, a large extinct mammal, which Scharf had to draw actual size. At 2 ft 3 in. it was the largest specimen he had every drawn on stone and it took him over 100 hours for which he charged £5. Unfortunately he had used an inferior stone and it printed so badly that Scharf felt obliged to draw it all over again for nothing. His conscientiousness did not pay him, however. A few months later Darwin became Secretary of the Geological Society and one of his first actions on taking office was to accuse Scharf of overcharging for his work.

Worse was to follow. When Scharf failed to deliver on time some work for the Geological Society and was rebuked by an official, Scharf told him 'that Artists ought not to be treated or spoken to like a common mechanic or servant – at which he felt offended and said that he should take good care that I should never draw for the Geological Society any more'.

The careers of Scharf's two sons, however, were progressing well. George jun., after a period at the Royal Academy School, went, in 1840, to Asia Minor as the official artist to Sir Charles Fellows's archaeological expedition and the drawings he made of views and antiquities of Lycia, Caria and Lydia were later published.[12] Henry was a totally different character. In 1841 he was appointed Articulator and General Assistant to the Museum of the College of Surgeons at a yearly salary of £100 but after almost two years wiring bones together Henry rebelled. He had already done some amateur dramatics; now he decided to try the stage professionally. He managed to secure six months engagement with a Mr Hall, lessee of the Newcastle Theatre, and on 5 November 1842 he set off. A few days later he wrote to his mother that he had 'very good cheap lodgings at 4s 6d a week 3rd floor at Mrs Simm's, Shakespeare St, near the theatre, and had good prospects'. After his Liverpool engagement Henry appeared at Sadler's Wells Theatre.[13]

On 20 October 1845 news came from Germany that Scharf's brother Joseph was dangerously ill and wanted to see him before he died. The next day, having packed twenty coloured drawings and 100 pencil drawings, he was on a steamship bound for Ostend, busily sketching until seasickness forced him to give up. Scharf arrived at his home town to find that his brother, who had been Burgomaster of Mainburg, had already died of cancer. In his will he left Scharf 4000 florins, half of which he received at once, the remainder he was to get on the death of Joseph's widow. This unexpected legacy enabled him to stay on in Germany for far longer than he could otherwise have done. He stayed, in fact, for two years. He worked as hard as ever. Writing home an account of a carnival in Munich he added: 'not that I joined in it, for I kept continually at home alone, drawing or writing'. He produced some notable work, mostly of Ratisbon, including a panorama from the top of the tower of the Golden Cross Inn, where he was staying, and a long view of the town from the other side of the Danube.[14] His money, however, did not go as far as he might have wished. Towards the end of his stay he had to leave the expensive Golden Cross and take two little rooms in a modest inn where even so, he could only afford his lodging without meals and he embarrassed his landlord by bringing his own bread and water into the restaurant.

In 1848, after Scharf's return to England, the family moved to 1 Torrington Square.[15] The new house with its many rates and taxes cost just under £150 per annum to run so George jun. must by now have taken over the financial responsibility of the family, for his father, finding it more difficult to get work and with his health beginning to fail, was never again to earn more than £100 a year. George jun. augmented the family income by giving lectures on Fine Art at his studio at home to ladies three times a week. Price 2½ guineas for a course of twenty lectures.

For the next few years Scharf helped his son by enlarging prints and by drawing diagrams for these lectures. He even tried his hand at designing wallpaper 'in destemper colours for block printing'. He was nothing if not versatile. But the poor reception of his paintings depressed him. Since his return, the Royal Academy had hung three of his German pictures but in 1852 he wrote of one which the Academy had rejected two years running. 'It disappointed me much,' he wrote, 'as I might have had a chance of selling it, and never yet, during 40 years, had I sold anything at an Exhibition.' This is one of the only occasions on which Scharf expresses the slightest complaint. It is from the diary of George jun. that we learn how he really felt: 'My father seems broken and discontented . . .'

In 1856 the lease on 1 Torrington Square had expired and although it could have been extended on a yearly basis, George jun. decided to move. The move, however, does not appear to have included his father. The reason for this strange situation is not clear. George jun. had not been very well and blamed his father for not paying him enough attention during his illness and also for not helping him with his lectures. Whatever the reason, George jun. took a house, 1 Eastcott Place, Camden Town, for himself and his mother and Aunt Mary.

George Scharf found lodgings in a first-floor front room at 37 Preston Street a short distance away. Perhaps he just wanted a little place of his own to work in because in the evenings he would walk to Eastcott Place to dine and sleep. He was quite happy in his little room for which he paid three shillings a week. 'It is a very pleasant situation with a Garden; and is only a threepenny ride in an Omnibus from Town,' and a stone's throw from the Newberry Arms public house[16] where he records paying 1s 10d for a pint of gin!

He was so short of money that he tried to sell some of his favourite German paintings. A large oil of the Walhalla near Ratisbon he put up

Mr Scharf's Residence.

Looking South, towards Keppel Street, from the left hand corner of Torrington Sqr.
9 Lamps on each side of the Sqr. to about 35 houses on each side.

J Scharf del 1850. Liberny. Lilac. Elm.
Plane, Lilac, Sycamore, Sycamore.

Trees at corner & Plain

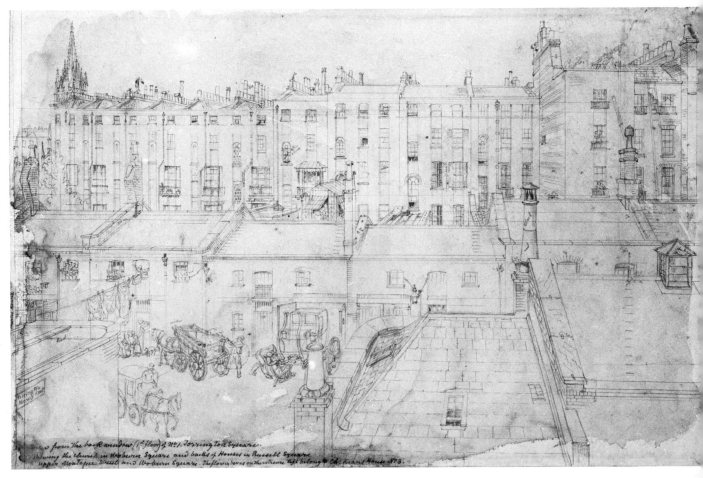

View from the back window (1st floor) of No 1. Torrington Square.
Shewing the elms in Woburn Square and backs of Houses in Russell Square
Upper Montague Street and Woburn Square. The flower boxes on the extreme left belong to Chimnet House 1843.

for auction at Robinson's Rooms at 21 Old Bond Street. It failed to get a single bid. A plan to dispose of it by lottery also failed and he finally let a Mr Edward Cock have it for £3.

In despair he went to his old customers, the City Corporation, and asked Mr Bunning, the City Architect, to propose to the Library Committee that they should buy some of his drawings. Bunning held out no hope that they would buy them 'for want of interest and want of money'.

On 14 July 1857 Scharf wrote to a Mr Boner asking him to send a petition to Prince Thurn und Taxis at Ratisbon. The petition stated his circumstances, the fact that he was not being provided for in his old age, and it asked for a pension in exchange for all his drawings. Boner, however, wrote back to say that he could not send the petition to the Prince – 'it being so strange to ask anyone for a Pension on whom one has no claim'.

Others were more helpful. Scharf's old employer, Professor Richard Owen, for whom he had worked for over twenty years, agreed to pay him a guinea a week for drawing anything he chose at the British Museum. This was no more than a charitable gesture by Owen who made it clear that Scharf would receive his payment no matter how little work he produced. Out of this he gave his wife 10 shillings a week for his laundry and evening meal.

Matters were made worse when, in April 1859, it was discovered that their old maidservant Ellen had been pocketing money meant for tradespeople. Some of them now sued Scharf in the County Court for payment of their bills. It appears that the only tradesman to insist on his rights was a baker who was awarded double the amount owed to him but Scharf was still ordered to pay the costs of the other plaintiffs. This was the last straw. A few weeks later Scharf, whose health had been declining steadily, now took to his bed with bronchitis. Luckily he had joined the Artists Amicable Fund as long ago as 1839 and he was now paid a pension of 30 shillings a week. He was attended by a Dr Sieveking, an amateur botanist, whom Scharf was able to pay by drawing diagrams for his lectures. The doctor advised him to avoid the open air and his health improved. But once more on his feet Scharf had to go all the way to 17 Manchester Square to obtain the doctor's signature on his health certificate so that he could get his pension. This, in the depths of winter, was too much. On 26 February 1860 his son wrote, 'Father very ill, confined to his bed, severe coughing.'

George jun. was by now the Secretary of the recently formed National Portrait Gallery with its headquarters at 29 Great George Street. This was a large four-storey building with apartments allocated for young George's private use. He asked his mother and his aunt to share the top flat with him but the invitation did not include his father.

However, he obviously could not be left alone while he was so ill and it was arranged that he should stay at Great George Street until he recovered. His health, however, did not improve and on 11 November 1860 George Scharf died. Four days later he was buried in Brompton Cemetery.

11 Scharf and his family moved into this corner house, No 1 Torrington Square, in 1849. This view, which he drew in 1850, is looking south towards Kepple Street in the background; on the left is the entrance to Torrington Mews East. London University buildings cover the whole area today

12 Torrington Mews East behind Scharf's house, No 1 Torrington Square. The view is looking north-east from one of his first-floor windows; in the background are the backs of the houses in Russell Square with the spire of Christchurch, Woburn Square, on the left

Notes

1 The fact that it was printed as an aquatint rather than a lithograph is not without significance. Although England was the first country outside Germany to have a lithographic press, nothing of any importance had yet been produced and interest in the new medium was at a very low ebb in 1818. Colnaghi probably had no faith in lithography and insisted on aquatint which was the most popular process for quality reproduction at the time. Scharf being unfamiliar with the medium was content to do the initial etching – the aquatinting (that is creating the tonal areas) was done by Robert Havell, one of the masters of the art.

2 Elizabeth Hicks was born on 1 August 1785 and died in January 1869. Mary Hicks died in March 1864 aged ninety.

3 St Martin-in-the-Fields Parish Register.

4 For his *St Giles* illustrations he charged £5 but was actually paid nothing. Instead he was given two books valued at a guinea.

5 Francis Street was re-named Torrington Place in 1938.

6 This old farmhouse was bought in 1840 by John Harris Heal, son of the founder of the famous furnishing business of Heal & Son Ltd – a business which was destined to expand throughout this whole block and lead to the demolition of that part of Francis Street which included George Scharf's house.

7 Richard Lambert Jones, died 16 August 1863, founder of the Guildhall Library.

8 George Scharf jun., in later life, was to become one of its Governors.

9 It is in Westminster Library, Archives Section, Buckingham Palace Road. Gardner Collection Box 57 No 7c.

10 The only known copy of this prospectus is in the Guildhall.

11 I have been unable to trace its present whereabouts, if indeed it exists. In the British Museum Department of Prints and Drawings is a large pencil-and-wash panoramic view from the roof of Westminster Hall. But it is quite crude and must be one of the preliminary sketches for the finished painting.

12 His subsequent career was one of great distinction. He wrote extensively on art and archaeology, advised Charles Kean on the correct costumes and scenery for his Shakespearian productions, and was one of the most active members of the Society of Antiquaries of which he was elected a fellow in 1852. He virtually created the National Portrait Gallery and became its first Director in 1882 increasing its paintings from 60 to 1000. Early in 1895 he was made a KCB but lived only a few weeks to enjoy his knighthood. He died, unmarried, on 19 April 1895 at 8 Ashley Place, Westminster.

13 After a moderately successful career on the London stage in minor roles, Henry was engaged by an American agent to appear in New York and Philadelphia. He left Liverpool on 20 July 1850 and settled permanently in the States. When not acting he gave English lessons to some Germans, travelled as a representative for the London publisher, John Tallis, and taught art and elocution at the Virginia Female Institute, Staunton. He died in America in about 1890.

14 Both now in the Department of Manuscripts at the British Museum.

15 No longer in existence – now covered by London University buildings.

16 Still standing at 40 Malden Road, London NW5.

I

ST MARTIN'S LANE
& CHARING CROSS

OLD CHARING CROSS

The area that was to become Trafalgar Square was originally occupied by the King's Mews, an open space flanked on the east, as far as the lower end of St Martin's Lane, by a clutter of stables, inns, barns and 'vile houses'. As early as 1812, John Nash's brave new architectural development linking Regent's Park with Carlton House had included a provision for 'a Square or Crescent open to and looking down Parliament Street – to be built round the equestrian statue at Charing Cross'. By 1825 Regent Street had been successfully built and Nash's plans for Charing Cross were revived. In the following year the Charing Cross Improvement Act was passed and newspapers and magazines were full of reports on the proposals. It was typical of Scharf to make a record of the existing buildings before they were torn down. If we are to believe Dr Johnson, 'the full tide of human existence is at Charing Cross'. When Scharf made this drawing (*right*) in 1825 it had changed very little from Johnson's day and the Doctor would have had no difficulty in recognising it. The low building on the left is an eighteenth-century tavern soon to be demolished. Two doors along, a coach is emerging from the yard of the Golden Cross Inn.

In the drawing (*far right*) made from the top of Whitehall, the steeple of St Martin-in-the-Fields can be seen above the roof-tops and the equestrian statue of Charles I also occupies the same position as it does today. The old tavern has been demolished and beyond the timber shoring can be seen the King's Mews stables and coach-houses built by William Kent in 1732. The turning round to the right leads to the Strand and the Golden Cross stands directly behind the Charles I statue.

A

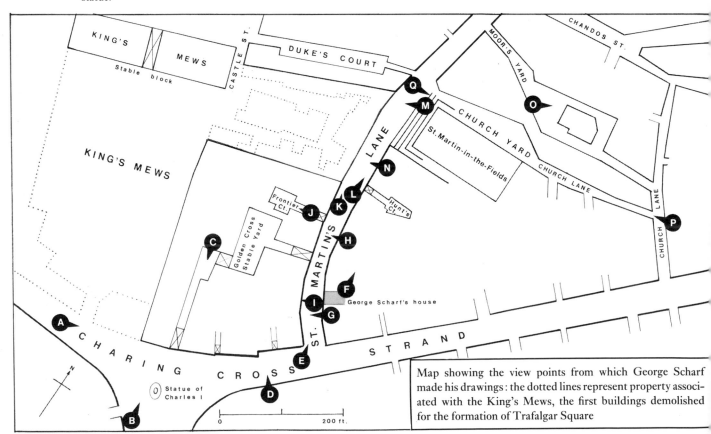

Map showing the view points from which George Scharf made his drawings: the dotted lines represent property associated with the King's Mews, the first buildings demolished for the formation of Trafalgar Square

B

GOLDEN CROSS COACH-YARD

Scharf's drawing (*right*) gives only the smallest idea of the vast area covered by the coach-yards and stabling of the Golden Cross Inn. This is merely the passage leading to the archway opening on to Charing Cross.

Through this entrance passed the 'Commodore' coach carrying Mr Pickwick and his friends to Rochester at the start of their travels. Mr Jingle's harrowing story of the tall lady whose head was knocked off by the low arch 'sandwich in her hand – no mouth to put it in – head of family off – shocking – shocking' was based on fact. The *Annual Register* reported on 11 April 1800, 'This afternoon, as the Chatham and Rochester coach came out of the gateway of the inn-yard of the Golden Cross, Charing Cross, a young woman, sitting on top, threw her head back, to prevent her from striking against the beam: but, there being so much luggage on the roof of the coach as to hinder her laying herself sufficiently back, it caught her face in a dreadful manner.' She died eight days later.

The archway on the left leads to a second, much bigger, yard with yet another opening on to St Martin's Lane (see p. 24).

C

Charing Cross in 1830 looking Northward

*Corner of St
Martin's Lane*

CHARING CROSS ⒟

Though this (*left*) would appear to be the beginning of the
Strand, the shops are actually Nos 1–9 Charing Cross. On
the extreme left is one of the strange Gothic-like pinnacles
of the Golden Cross. No 9 next door was for years famous
as the Lottery Office of Thomas Bish but lotteries had been
abolished four years before this drawing was made in 1830
and No 9 was now sub-let to a tea merchant. At No 4 is the
Northumberland Coffee House down the side of which runs
Chequers Court named after an Elizabethan inn which stood
on this site. Next door is John Dobree, the pawnbroker; John
Pauli, a furrier; and Samuel Belcher, linen-draper, at No 1
on the corner of St Martin's Lane.

ST MARTIN'S LANE

Below left we see Belcher's shop again a few months later
when the east side of St Martin's Lane is being demolished.
The Army & Navy was a coffee house run by John Jagger
and next door, at No 3, was George Scharf's home. Here he
married Elizabeth Hicks and here their two sons were born.
On the door which led upstairs to his rooms he has put a
notice announcing that he has moved to 14 Francis Street.

In 1826, in anticipation of this whole block vanishing under
the pick-axe, Scharf made a drawing (*below*) of the roof-tops
behind his house in St Martin's Lane with the steeple of St
Martin-in-the-Fields in the background.

G H

ST MARTIN'S LANE: West

Thanks to George Scharf we have a record of nearly every building that was demolished in the southern part of St Martin's Lane. The numbering began on the south-east corner and ran consecutively up to Long Acre then continued down the west side to end at No 149. Today's numbering remains the same so that, with the southern half cut off to make Trafalgar Square, St Martin's Lane now begins at No 29 and ends at No 110. Scharf's drawing of the west side (*top right*) begins at Solomon's Goldsmith & Silversmith, at No 137 and ends at Moyes the Baker at No 147. The archway between the two bollards is another access to the stable yard of the Golden Cross (see p. 21). For some reason Scharf did not continue down to the Strand. Luckily his son George jun. made a watercolour of this missing section when he was only nine years old and in 1864 he copied it in pen and ink (*top left*) for his friend John Edmund Gardner, the great London collector.

George sen. did, however, make this careful watercolour (*left*) of No 148, the shop of Alexander McNab, Surgeon and Apothecary.

FRONTIER COURT

The other archway leads to Frontier Court (see also p. 28) which was occupied by the premises of Hayward & Nixon, Builders and Carpenters (*right*). After their demolition they moved to Palace New Road, Lambeth, with a West End office at 22 Leicester Square where they remained until 1866. During this time one of their contracts was for Batty's Hippodrome. Beneath the building behind the chimney on the left was 'Queen Elizabeth's Bath'. According to antiquarians who examined it just before its demolition it was constructed of red brick and dated from the fifteenth century.

I

J

FURTHER UP ST MARTIN'S LANE

These two drawings, both dated 1825, show the view further up St Martin's Lane. On the west side (*above*), numbered 1 to 6 by Scharf, are the backs of the buildings whose entrances were in the King's Mews. They were soon to be demolished to make the opening seen on p. 29. That numbered 1 is the back of an ancient ale-house called the Barn which must have led to confusion since directly across the road was another pub called the Old Barn. At 6 is the St Martin's Watch House where a couple are looking through a grille into the cells. The Watch House once had an entrance in St Martin's Lane but in 1742 an enraged mob tore down the front after some drunken constables had crammed twelve women into the tiny prison overnight and six had died. Presumably as a result of this incident a new entrance was made on the King's Mews side where stricter vigilance could be maintained. The rest of these buildings were occupied by Crown Servants attached to the Mews. On the extreme left a man is looking in the window of Solomon's the Goldsmith at No 137 which is the shop where Scharf began his drawing on the previous page.

The viewpoint in the drawing on the *right* shifts slightly further west and shows the extent to which St Martin's Church was hemmed in on all sides. The lamp post is the same in both drawings. After the Watch House on the left, the numbering moves to No 134, Blake the Haberdasher, a building which probably dates back to the seventeenth century. Three doors along is the entrance to Duke's Court which leads to Castle Street. Across the road the brick wall surmounted by railings jutting out beyond St Martin's portico encloses St Martin's burial ground. This was removed to make way for Duncannon Street. Vaults were created at the east end of the church to receive the disturbed remains and a new cemetery for future burials was opened in Pratt Street, Camden Town. At the extreme right is the entrance to Hunt's Court described in 1720 by Strype as a 'pretty handsome square Court, with five or six good built and inhabited Houses, with a Door at the Entrance, to shut up at Nights, for the Security of its Inhabitants'. By the time of their demolition, however, the network of alleys and courts between the church and the Strand had degenerated into some of the worst slums in this part of London, but Hunt's Court still appears to retain a certain privacy for its residents with the iron gate at its entrance.

GENESIS OF
TRAFALGAR SQUARE

As early as 1734, the architectural critic James Ralph suggested that the clutter of buildings in front of St Martin-in-
the-Fields should be removed to open up an uninterrupted
view of the church. The idea was revived by John Nash who
allowed for just such a scheme as part of his Metropolitan
Improvements. With Regent Street finished it was time to
carry out 'the continuation of Pall Mall into St Martin's Lane,
terminating at the Portico of St Martin's Church'. The Act
authorising this much-needed improvement was passed on
31 May 1826; by August of that year George Scharf was able
to stand on the steps of St Martin's and make the drawing
(*right*). The long-awaited opening up had indeed been
achieved. It was now possible to see as far as Pall Mall where
the colonnade juts out in front of the Opera House,
Haymarket. The future Trafalgar Square begins to take shape
with the appearance of its first building – the College of Physicians with its classical portico still standing today. On the
right is one of the cupolas of the King's Mews, the stables
designed by Kent in 1732 which approximates to the site of
the National Gallery. The miscellany of buildings on the left,
typical of the 'vile houses' which once obstructed the view,
are part of the old barracks and the backs of Hayward & Nixon's premises (see p. 25). On the corner we have a rare view
of a three-door public privy.

A year later and some more mews buildings have gone
revealing (*right*) the backs of all the houses on the south side
of Duke's Court. This was a wide and important court of
some dozen houses running between St Martin's Lane and
Castle Street the southern end of which can be seen in the
centre of the drawing where it runs past the blank side wall
of Kent's King's Mews. The corner building on the extreme
right is No 134 St Martin's Lane, Blake the Haberdasher,
last seen on p. 26 next to the Watch House. Everything on
the right was soon to be demolished to make way for the
National Gallery.

... the steps of St Martin Church, august 1826

from the steps of St Martin Church — 1827

MOOR'S YARD

The entrance to Moor's Yard (*right*) was north of St Martin's Church between Nos 23 & 24 on the east side of St Martin's Lane. In Strype's *Survey* of 1720, he describes it as 'a large Place for Stablings, with several ordinary Houses, and has a Passage into Church Lane'. Although it began as a narrow alley from St Martin's Lane, it soon spread out into an open space almost the size of St Martin's Church. In the middle of the open space was an isolated block clearly seen towards the right. This probably occupies the site of the horsepond which was there in the eighteenth century. It was always associated with horses. There was a farrier here in 1683 and the last occupant of Moor's Yard, as late as 1839, was John Armstrong, Farrier. Eastward from Scharf's drawing Moor's Yard narrowed again into a long alleyway which ended at Church Lane.

O

P

CHURCH LANE

Behind St Martin's Church was a squalid labyrinth of courts and alleys and the Elizabethans, with their love of nicknames and word play, called this area the Bermudas. For it was then the extremity of town, as far west as any Londoner would wish to travel, and its circuitous lanes weaving around islands of shoddy tenements, of which Moor's Yard was a typical example, could be compared to the narrow and intricate channels surrounding the islands of Bermuda. Church Lane (*far left*) had an entrance from the Strand and ran north up to Chandos Street. But about half-way up before the junction with Moor's Yard, a branch, still called Church Lane, ran westwards to Church Yard. Scharf was standing at this junction looking towards the back of St Martin's Church when he made this drawing in 1828. Coutts's Bank now occupies the site.

CHURCH YARD

Back in St Martin's Lane (*left*) as we look along the stepped portico of St Martin's Church we can see the other end of Church Lane as it emerges into the open paved area called Church Yard. It was dubbed Porridge Island because of the number of cook-shops here and the name persisted up to the time all these buildings were demolished. Those on the left were replaced by the Vicar's House, the Vestry Room and the National School – buildings which remain virtually unaltered to this day. Behind St Martin's a roadway, Adelaide Street, was cut through to the Strand. This was recently closed to traffic to become a paved area for pedestrians once again.

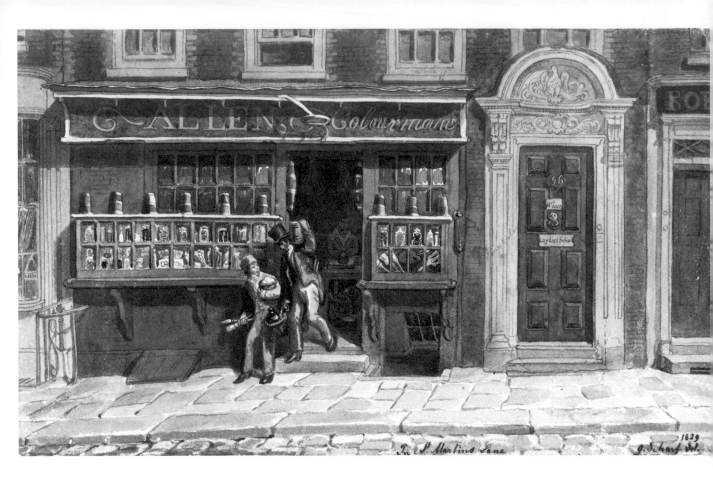

ALLEN'S

No 96 St Martin's Lane, on the west side, four doors south of Cecil Court, had an interesting history. To judge from its ornate Queen Anne door frame, heavily carved with spread eagle and foliage, it was built as a private house around 1700. Its most famous resident was Dr Misaubin who died here on 20 April 1734. He was a Frenchman who graduated MD in France in 1687 and was granted a licence to practise in London by the College of Physicians in 1719. Though a qualified doctor, his selling of patent medicines, particularly his famous anti-venereal pill, caused him to be branded a quack, so that when Hogarth wanted a typical quack doctor for his third plate of *Marriage à la Mode*, it was Dr Misaubin he used as a model. After his death, his widow continued to sell the famous pill.

The interior of the house must have been impressive. It had a large staircase painted with figures viewing a procession which Dr Misaubin had commissioned from the French pain-

ter, Clermont, who charged 1000 guineas for the work but who settled for 500. The ground floor was converted into a shop some time in the late eighteenth century for it was an Oil and Colourman's as early as 1794 when it was occupied by one Edward Powell. His mother, every year, made a pipe of wine (some 100 gallons) from a vine nearly 100 ft long presumably in their back garden.

By 1829, when George Scharf made this watercolour, the shop had been taken over by Edward Prascey Allen. As it was the nearest colourman's shop to Scharf's house just down St Martin's Lane, it is not too fanciful to suggest that he depicted himself leaving it with his eldest son George.

The door by the side of the shop led to a school run by Sarah Watts. It was still a school in 1868 although the shop had become a woollen warehouse but in the 1880s it was demolished and today its site is covered by the entrance to Burleigh Mansions.

In the Streets of London
Drawn from Nature by G. Scharf

2

IN THE STREETS
OF LONDON

STREET ADVERTISING

George Scharf's arrival in London coincided with some revolutionary ideas which heralded the dawning of modern advertising. Londoners were accustomed to seeing every blank wall or empty shop plastered over with posters, and the wooden hoardings which sprang up around the new building sites and improvements were an open invitation to the bill-stickers. To this army of so-called external paper-hangers was added an innovation which William Weir, writing for Knight's *London* in 1843, called 'peripatetic placards'. Weir compared them to Roman standard-bearers and said that they were a comparatively recent invention. Scharf was attracted as much by their outlandish clothes as their 'standards' and he gathered them together in colourful groups painted from sketches he had made over a period of twenty years.

A novelty which was finally to oust the standard-bearer was what Weir described as 'a heraldic anomaly, with placards hanging down before and behind like a herald's tabard'. It was the brilliant imagery of Charles Dickens, who likened this phenomenon to 'a piece of human flesh between two slices

of paste board', which gave us the 'sandwich man'. The earliest example depicted by George Scharf was sketched in 1828; he is seen (*above*) advertising the Battles of the French Army being shown at the Egyptian Hall, Piccadilly. Also shown (*top right*) is a variant in the form of a very mock turtle advertising, not soup, but port wine.

Belzoni's Exhibition (*bottom right*) caused a sensation. Giovanni Battista Belzoni was a 6ft 6in. Italian strongman and sideshow performer who went to Egypt on an abortive business trip, became fascinated with its antiquities, and ended his life as a world-renowned Egyptologist. He gathered together a notable collection of artefacts which he shipped to England in 1820 and exhibited at the Egyptian Hall, Piccadilly, the one place in London which, with its appropriate name and façade, might have been specially made for such a show. It opened to the public on 1 May 1821 and stimulated an interest in Egyptology among a general public which had previously known almost nothing about that ancient civilisation. The show ran for over a year, closing in June 1822.

ANATOMICAL MODEL of the Human Figure

GIRAFFES
at the SURREY ZOOLOGICAL GARDENS and Regent Street

LINEN DRAPER HABERDASHER SILKS CAMBRIC

GRIL AND SON WOOD LETTERS manufacturers

GRIL AND SON WOOD LETTERS Manufactory 2, Porter Street NEWPORT St NEWPORT MARKET

old PORT WINE

CATLIN'S INDIAN EXHIBITION EGYPTIAN HALL 500 PORTRAITS Dresses, Scalps Wigwams Admission one shilling

in Regents Street 1834. 2 1836 3 —39. 4 —40. 5 July 1840 6

Westminster ELECTION
Burdett 2171
Romilly 2546
Maxwell 2169
Hunt 58
1818

CITY ELECTION 1818 Last days Poll
WOOD 5700
WILSON 4824
WAITHMAN 4603
THORP 4335
CURTIS 4224
ATKINS 4688

LOTTERY 1824
FOUR
£20.000
£20.000
£20.000
£20.000
HAZARD & Cornhill

BELZONI'S EGYPTIAN TOMB at the EGYPTIAN HALL Piccadilly. open from 11 to 6 admittance one Shilling

EXHIBITION OF THE SOCIETY of BRITISH ARTISTS Suffolk Street

A MODEL of PALESTINE Exhibiting in ADAM Street Adelphi

1818 before 1825. —21. —23. about 1824 Look to the back

ADVERTISING GALORE

William Weir, writing in Knight's *London*, observed that when individual placard-carriers 'had ceased to be novelties and consequently, to attract attention, some brilliant genius conceived the idea of reviving their declining powers by the simple process of multiplication'. Here (*above*) the enterprising proprietors of the *Weekly Chronicle* in 1836 not only multiply their board-carriers but throw in a mobile band to advertise their free gift of a print of the famous Nassau Balloon.

The board with hats sticking out of it (*below*) was an obvious device for advertising 'Hat Pictures in Great Variety' but as to what they were, one can only speculate. Printed calendars made specifically to stick inside top hats were well known and they probably gave some enterprising printer the idea for producing pictures less useful but more amusing for the Victorian gentleman to keep under his hat. The walking advertisement for waterproof boots must have caught the eye; the boots are immersed in a tank of water.

The impressive standard-bearer and his companion (*right*) advertised a Diorama depicting the second funeral of Napoleon in Paris. It was shown in 1841 at the St James's Bazaar, which stood on the corner of King Street and St James's Street. Scharf noted that 'it was very Fine' and although the five scenes were painted by 'The Board of Arts for the Ceremony' – whoever they were – and the exhibition was accompanied by funeral music composed by Auber, it was not a success.

Warren's Blacking was one of the most widely advertised commodities in the 1830s and there was hardly a single newspaper that did not carry their comic rhyming adverts. Robert Warren of 30 Strand, who claimed to be the inventor of Japan Liquid Blacking, was one of the pioneers of 'display' advertising using woodcuts usually showing reflections in a highly polished boot, and the walking tins of blacking (*below*) is just another example of his marketing ideas. Unfortunately there was then no copyright protection and a rival firm of the same name took full advantage of Robert Warren's advertising. Their address was 30 Hungerford Stairs, Strand, and by printing their pot labels with the words Hungerford Stairs very small and Warren, 30 and Strand very large, they hoped that their blacking would be mistaken for the better known brand. It was for this rival 'Warren's' that the twelve-year-old Charles Dickens spent a miserable six months in 1824 sticking labels on blacking pots in the warehouse at Hungerford Stairs.

VEHICULAR PLACARDS

In the great battle of advertising, the army of board-carriers
were the infantry, but some enterprising advertisers threw
in the cavalry in the form of horse-drawn carts surmounted
by monstrous models of their products such as top hats, boots,
tea caddies, sometimes with the driver hidden inside. Once
these unwieldy juggernauts caught on, they began to clutter
up the roads to such an extent that they were expressly forbidden in the Hackney & Stage Carriage Act of 1853. Charles
Dickens, while contributing to *Household Words* in 1851,
actually conducted an interview inside one of these monstrosi-
ties as it trundled along Cornhill. 'It was a new sensation',
he wrote, 'to be jolting through the tumult of the city in that
secluded Temple, partly open to the sky, surrounded by the
roar without, and seeing nothing but the clouds. Occasionally,
blows from whips fell heavily on the Temple's walls, when
by stopping up the road longer than usual, we irritated carters
and coachmen to madness; but they fell harmless upon us
within and disturbed not the serenity of our peaceful retreat.'
Scharf's pencil sketches of the 1840s (*above*) show a gigantic
coffee-mill, a coal stove, and an extraordinary construction
with a giant telescope at each corner advertising an optician.

In Oxford Street
March 1843
G.S.

TRAVELLING SHOWS

In addition to the exhibitions regularly put on at the numerous halls and galleries of London, there was no shortage of small mobile sideshows travelling round the streets. One of the humblest must have been the stuffed alligator 'just arrived from Egypt' in its coffin-like cart (*top left*) which Scharf saw in Upper St Martin's Lane in 1845 Viewed by one customer at a time, it cost a penny a look. The 'Savages Eating Raw Flesh and the Human Boy all overgrown with Hair' (*bottom left*) were probably fakes to deceive the gullible, but there is no doubt that the show above was genuine enough to satisfy the public's morbid curiosity. Scharf drew it in Oxford Street in 1845 but makes no comment; perhaps he was too sensitive to gape at the fat lady or 'the most wonderful sight, a boy born without arms and hands' (*above*). Scharf saw Wombwell's Royal Menagerie (*right*) at Bartholomew Fair which was held in Smithfield every year until 1855. George Wombwell, one of the greatest showmen of the age, travelled the country with his caravans of wild animals and 'did more', said the obituary in *The Times*, 'to forward practically the study of natural history among the masses' than anyone before.

FANTOCCINI

The drawings on these pages are of a long-forgotten street entertainment which, for a time, threatened to oust the Punch & Judy show although William Hone, who saw it in 1826, thought otherwise. 'Our old acquaintance "Punch" will survive all this,' he wrote.

Fantoccini was a portable marionette theatre, tall enough to allow the standing puppeteer to manipulate his string-puppets from above in contrast to the Punch & Judy man who worked his glove-puppets from below. According to a Fantoccini man interviewed by Henry Mayhew, it was a Scotsman named Gray who first introduced this kind of show onto the London streets in the 1820s, though it may have been slightly earlier. He was later engaged to perform at Vauxhall Gardens at £10 a week. Mayhew's man was also doing very well thirty years later with crowds following him around 'like flies after honey', taking '18s 6d in half an hour corner-pitching'. He was always accompanied by a man to play the drum and pan pipes (*above & left*), whom he was able to pay 'an average as good as 4s a day'. 'If I'm very lucky,' he said, 'I makes it better for him, for a man can't be expected to go and blow his life away into a pandean pipe unless he's well paid for it.'

FANTASINA

mantle
yellow

dark blue
with red

A very ingenious contrivance, I saw it on Tower Hill about 1819

the Kelidascop 1820

INGENIOUS CONTRIVANCES

The streets of early nineteenth-century London were an open-air theatre of pavement shows, mostly crude, home-made constructions which nevertheless displayed enough novel ingenuity to entice the curious to part with their pennies.

'A very ingenious contrivance' is Scharf's description of the show (*top left*) which he saw on Tower Hill about 1819. It appears to be a tableau of small mechanical figures all made to perform their individual actions by the turning of a handle at the back.

The Kaleidoscope was invented by Sir David Brewster and widely pirated before he took out a patent in 1817. 'The sensation it excited in London throughout all ranks of people was astonishing,' ran one contemporary account. 'Kaleidoscopes were manufactured in immense numbers, and were sold as rapidly as they could be made. Dr Brewster states that no fewer than 200,000 kaleidoscopes were sold in London and Paris in the space of three months.' No record of it ever having been adapted as a street entertainment appears to exist. However, Scharf's rough sketch of 1820 (*bottom left*) is clearly captioned 'the Kelidascop' though how it works is not clear. Each individual viewing tube seems to have contained the necessary optics and the light obviously entered through the top of the drum which must have held some colourful material. Perhaps it was candle-lit at night with the lid down.

Peepshows were among the commonest of street entertainments. Some were small enough to be carried on the show-man's back, others (*top right*) were big enough to be drawn by a donkey. They took various forms. In the simplest form the viewer or viewers, according to the number of eyepieces, would be shown historical events or sensational episodes of contemporary life in a succession of scenes let down from above or inserted from the side. More elaborate ones used mirrors and optical tricks to add depth and perspective. Scharf's example shows his wife and two sons enjoying the Battle of Waterloo.

Scharf wrote under the drawing (*bottom right*) 'The Coach and Animals walk round the Table', without any attempt at an explanation. Later Mayhew was to interview an Italian who put on a very similar show with clockwork figures he had imported from Germany. 'They perform on the round table,' he said, 'which must be level or they will not turn round.' He showed Mayhew a carriage which 'will run round the table, and the horses will move as if they gallop – I attach this wire from the front wheel to the centre of the table, or it would run off the side and break itself.' He, too, was accompanied by a hurdy-gurdy man who played in time with the figures, slowing down as the clockwork slowed down.

43

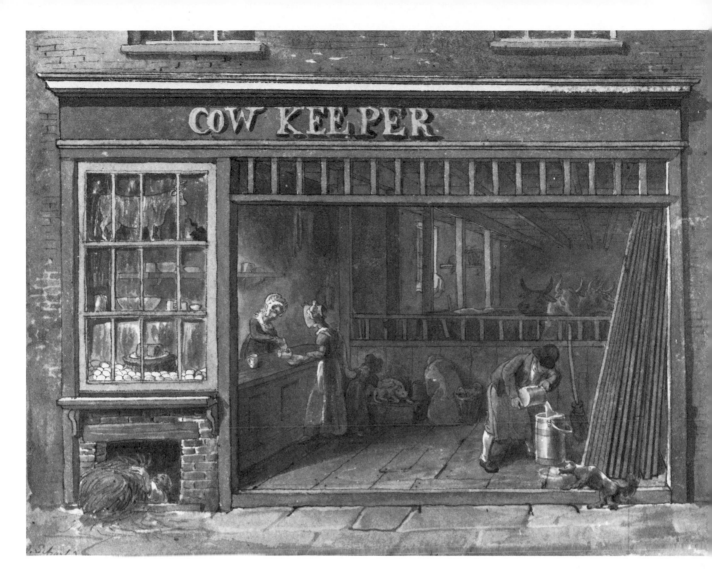

LONDON'S MILK

'This I drew in Golden Lane in the City in order to compare it with an elegant milk shop in the Quadrant, Piccadilly,' wrote Scharf in 1825 of the watercolour *above*. He could not have chosen a greater contrast. Golden Lane, which ran between Old Street and Barbican, was one of the most disreputable parts of the City. When Charles Dickens asked a local police inspector to show him a typical thieves' district he was shown Golden Lane and its immediate surroundings.

The Regent Street Quadrant (*left*), on the other hand, had been built only five years before and was all charm and elegance. Ironically, milk from the Golden Lane cow-keeper, with his little herd of cows in the back-yard, was probably fresher than that bought from the Quadrant shop which had to rely on delivery from a distant dairy.

Cow-keeping was a very profitable trade. Only in dairies on the edge of town were cows put out to grass: the metropolitan ones never saw a meadow. They were confined to stalls and exercised in stone-flagged yards. Their food consisted of grain, 45 quarters per week to every 25 cows, given to them twice a day, which was supplemented with turnips and one truss of hay shared between 10 cows. Each cow yielded an average of nine quarts of milk a day.

The cow-keeper did not even milk his own cows. It was the custom for the retailers to contract for the milk from a certain number of cows which were milked by their own milkmaids who carried it off for sale.

'MILK-O'

In 1818, when Scharf painted this watercolour (*above*), milk-men were a rarity; a far more common sight in London's streets was the ubiquitous milkmaid. A contemporary writer gave a graphic description of the hard life they led: 'The milk is conveyed from the cow-house in tin pails, which are principally carried by strong, robust Welsh girls, but a considerable number of Irish women are also employed for this purpose. These are the same that retail the milk about the streets of the Metropolis; and it is amazing to witness the labour and fatigue these females will undergo, and the hilarity and cheerfulness that prevails among them, and which tends, in a surprising manner, to lighten their laborious employment. Even in the most inclement weather, and in the depths of winter, they arrive in parties from different parts of the Metropolis, by three or four o'clock in the morning, laughing and singing to the music of their empty pails: with these they return loaded to town; and the weight they are thus accustomed to carry on their yokes, for a distance of two or three miles, is sometimes from 100 to 130 pounds.'

This was only their morning round. By midday they had returned to the cow-keepers' for more milking after which they were back on the streets until six in the evening. For this they were paid nine shillings a week with breakfast thrown in. The milkmaid often had a round of regular customers, or 'milk walk', which was jealously guarded and sometimes changed hands for considerable sums of money.

Some were itinerants who 'cried their milk' looking for casual buyers. Their cry of 'Milk below' became corrupted to 'Mio' which some wag interpreted as 'mi-eau' – half water, a reference to the fact that it was common practice to dilute the milk. According to *The Picture of London for 1819* the customer had to pay double what the milk cost and 'not content with this profit the retailers add water to the milk, to the extent, on the average, of a sixth part'.

Cow yards had water pumps for the express purpose of diluting the milk. One actually had a name, the Black Cow, 'from its being painted of that colour; and it is said to yield more than all the rest put together'.

DAILY DELIVERY

The streets of London rang with the cries of itinerant traders selling all manner of things but regular customers could also have goods delivered to their doors. Here (*right*) the butcher and the baker make their daily deliveries at a house in Francis Street, possibly Scharf's own house, in 1833 when he was living there.

BAKERS' CARTS

Since 1822 bread had to be sold in the Metropolis by weight, and to avoid short measure, for which bakers were notorious, the law required that delivery boys should be supplied with weights and scales.

There is no evidence of them in Scharf's drawings (*below*) of bakers' carts but he was clearly intrigued by their variety.

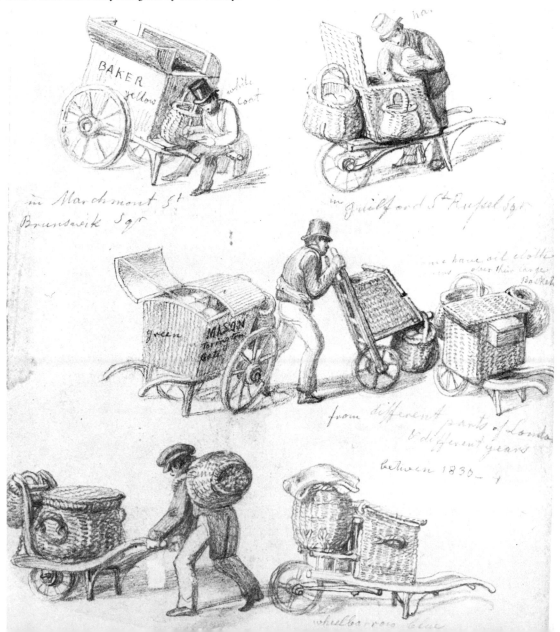

UMBRELLA PRINTS

'Here is a motley collection of prints,' declared the *Illustrated London News* in 1851, 'a wondrous gallery of art.' It had to admit, however, that 'the gratuitous illustrations issued by newspaper proprietors have done great harm' to the street-sellers of prints. In fact it killed a trade which had been flourishing for many years. The 'prints' were mostly illustrations from magazines, annuals and part-works which had been torn out by waste-paper collectors who then sold them in bulk to special 'swag-shops' before disposing of the rest of the paper for pulping. The umbrella print man (*top left*), according to Mayhew, bought them for about 5d a dozen and sold them for a penny or a halfpenny. He interviewed 'a little old man who used to have a print umbrella in the New Cut' who explained that sometimes the prints were resting on tapes attached to the ribs of the umbrella and sometimes they were pinned to the silk: 'I use werry fine pins, though they's dearer.' The trade could be pursued only in dry weather and he had to keep a look-out for approaching rain. 'Many's the time them devils o' boys has come up to me and has said "It'll thunder in five minutes, old bloke, so hup with yer humbereller, and go 'ome; hup with it just as it is; it'll show stunnin'; and sell as yer goes."'

HOUSEHOLD GOODS

There was no limit to the variety of goods that were sold in the streets by itinerant vendors. On the *left* the boy carries footstools, the man has ladies' embroidery frames and the woman clothes-horses.

Above are more footstools, 'shoes made from carpet of different colours' (the original carpet slippers), sieves, and tin ware (the device in the man's left hand is a roasting frame to hook on to the fire-grate). The broom-seller and the chair-mender show great ingenuity in their carrying methods and the last vendor is selling hot pies.

50

Handwritten annotations in the illustration:
light blue
Biscuits and sweet cakes
Tins
This stand is made of Iron & Tin, and gingerbread kept hot in it
in Charing Cross: between 1820 — 30.

FLOWERS & FRUIT

Here Scharf has gathered together on one sheet (*left*) a variety of flowers and fruit and has noted the months when these seasonal commodities were sold. Strawberries had the shortest season. They were sold only in June in small cone-shaped baskets called pottles seen being carried by the woman and her child. In the early nineteenth century they were expensive at around sixpence a pottle which held a little less than a quart. There was an additional charge of a penny on the pottle returnable if the customer brought back the little basket.

HOT FOOD

One man (*above*) sells biscuits and sweet cakes and another sells gingerbread kept hot in his little charcoal-burning tin stove.

By far the most popular of the hot food sold in the street was the baked potato, sold from specially made cans like the one being carried (*right*). These cans, either hired or bought outright by the vendor, were ingenious contrivances. Underneath was a charcoal fire-pot which heated the water in one half of the can, the steam being released through a safety-valve in the lid. The potatoes were put in the other side of the can already cooked and hot. Outside were two compartments, one for the butter and salt, the other for fresh charcoal.

Old Chairs to mend

white jaket

blue coat red wiestcoat

J. Scharf del

1820—30

CHAIRS TO MEND

Owing to the difficulty of getting rushes from Holland during the Napoleonic wars the once-popular rush-seated chair had, by George Scharf's time, been largely replaced by cane. The seats not only wore out quickly but were easily damaged and the itinerant chair-mender (*left*) became a common sight in the streets of London.

He also featured in books of trades and street cries and in children's chap-books which never missed an opportunity to preach to their little readers. One of 1828 asks, 'Has every chair which wants a new bottom been worn out fairly? Have no little boys or great girls been standing up on them?'

Scharf's drawings show how the canes and reeds were carried, and his eye for detail reveals that the canes could be scraped with a knife as the man at the bottom is doing or, like the man on the left, a special tool could be used.

SAWS TO FILE

The man (*right*), painted in 1840, is filing a saw and must have carried around with him a portable vice which he could rest against a lamppost.

KNIVES TO GRIND

The itinerant knife-grinder (*above*) had been a common sight in the streets of London since the seventeenth century and was still plying his trade within living memory.

Each knife-grinder made his own machine, ingenious devices of treadles and wheels turning a grindstone kept wet by water steadily dripping from the little barrel above it.

The World in Miniature, published in 1827, gives their charges: table-knives 3 shillings a dozen, carving-knives 4d each and scissors 3d. The same anonymous author added, rather sourly, 'some of these itinerants earn more by their promiscuous employment in one day, than a ploughman by his steady labours in a week'.

STREET MUSIC

The streets of George Scharf's London were filled with the sound of music. The performers (*above*) look proficient enough and were probably musicians eking out a living between professional engagements in concert hall or theatre pit. These would have been tolerated and even encouraged by some, but others found all street music an insufferable nuisance. Early in Queen Victoria's reign an Act of Parliament gave residents the power to insist that street musicians should go away in cases of 'illness or other reasonable cause'. This clause led to such misinterpretation that the Act had to be tightened up in 1864 and is still in force.

ORGAN GRINDERS

Among the street noises which induced Thomas Carlyle to build a sound-proof room on top of his house in Cheyne Row, Chelsea, were the '"vile yellow Italians" grinding under his windows'. The instrument they were grinding had to be either the hurdy-gurdy or the barrel-organ. The hurdy-gurdy being played by boys (*below*) was quite a serious instrument requiring some skill. The handle turned a rosined wheel rubbing against strings which produced notes when the piano-like finger keys were depressed. The other 'grinding' instrument was the barrel-organ (*bottom left*). This required no skill at all but was merely a revolving drum studded with pins which opened valves in organ pipes blown by the bellows worked off the grinding handle. Later in the century, both the names hurdy-gurdy and barrel-organ were colloquially applied to the street piano which, within living memory, superseded the old instruments in London's streets.

a blind man

ONE-MAN BAND

As the panpipes, at this time commonly called the mouth-organ, could be played without the use of hands, the musician was able to play another instrument at the same time, usually a drum. The combination was ideal for the one-man band. Scharf's example (*above*) also plays an ingenious hat of bells.

Far more ingenious examples of the one-man band are seen on the *right*. Remarkably both drawings, the top dated 1833 and the bottom 1843, could depict the same man. Even more remarkably he is almost certainly the man Mayhew interviewed in about 1850. 'I have been blind since within a month of my birth,' he said, 'and have been 23 years a street performer. My parents were poor, but managed to have me taught music. I am 55 years old. I started the bells that I play now, as near as I can recollect, some 18 years ago. When I first played them, I had my 14 bells arranged on a rail, and tapped them with my two leather hammers held in my hands in the usual way. I thought next I could introduce some novelty into the performance. The novelty I speak of was to play the violin with the bells. I had hammers fixed on a rail, so as each bell had its particular hammer; these hammers were connected with cords to a pedal acting with a spring to bring itself up, and so, by playing the pedal with my feet, I had full command of the bells, and made them accompany the violin, so that I could give any tune almost with the power of a band. I played the violoncello with my feet also, on a plan of my own, and the violin in my hand. I had the violoncello on a frame on the ground, so arranged that I could move the bow with my foot in harmony with the violin in my hand.'

blind man

g. Scharf

a yellowish grey silk cloak

SPARE A COPPER

The wandering barrel-organ woman with her little family and the enterprising crippled trumpeter in his ingenious dog-cart would have had no difficulty in eliciting anyone's sympathy, but Scharf was somewhat suspicious of the sailor with the model ship on his head whom he drew on two different occasions. He wrote ' I saw him the first time in Russell Sq. 1840 and several times since during about 10 years, *the Child being always the same.*'

I saw him the first time in Russ ✗ *Squ 1840. and several times since g. S*

white with brown

London

3

STRAND

HUNGERFORD MARKET – OLD

Hungerford Market was named after Sir Edward Hungerford on whose land it was built in 1682 to sell fruit and vegetables as a rival to Covent Garden. But it was a failure. The market house became a school then a French chapel and by the beginning of the nineteenth century the whole site had become run-down and squalid.

In spite of its previous failure, the Hungerford Market Company was formed in 1830, and Charles Fowler, the architect who had just finished Covent Garden Market, was invited to design the new buildings. The drawing *below*, dated March 1832 and looking south towards the river, shows the old market buildings being demolished while through the stone gateway the new building is taking shape. The keystone of the gateway bears the crest of Hungerford, a wheatsheaf between two sickles rising from a ducal coronet. On the right, the pub and fishmongers are part of old Hungerford Street which runs up to the Strand.

– AND NEW

Four months later (*right*) from the same viewpoint but a little higher, the pub and fishmongers in Hungerford Street are still standing though everything else has gone and the new market is rising rapidly.

The columns in the foreground will form the entrance to the Great Hall, 188 ft long by 123 ft wide, while the completed towers behind are actually on the riverside wharf. Excavations in the foreground will lead to a double range of arched cellars or vaults opening on to a fish market which, it was hoped, would rival Billingsgate. Shops were built along both sides of the hall and in the galleries above, while the floor space was left clear for casual stall holders.

The whole building was quite splendid. It was opened on 2 July 1833 with a balloon ascent and a fireworks display in the evening.

However, like its predecessor, it failed and the whole site was cleared in 1862 to make way for Charing Cross Station.

CORNER SHOP

'Houses building at the corner of Hungerford Street leading
to Hungerford Market August 1834' reads Scharf's caption
to this drawing (*right*).

When Hungerford Street led from the Strand to the old
market it was little more than a narrow lane. As the grand
entry to the new market it was widened to 30 ft with new
shops and houses on either side. The north-west corner, here
being erected using the new building methods incorporating
cast-iron girders, became No 20 Strand and, when finished,
was occupied by W. Marshall, Tea Dealer and Grocer.

STRAND : South Side

It is early morning and the shops are just opening (*above*).
An assistant from the emporium of John Fox, Perfumer &
Hairdresser, sweeps the pavement while his colleague lays the
dust with the aid of a watering can. Next door at No 71 a
shop-boy is taking in the last of the panels with which the
windows had been boarded up over night; No 71 is basically
a seventeenth-century building of red brick illustrating the
extraordinary mixture of architectural styles which distinguished the Strand.

  The end building, No 72, Benstead & Norton, Hosiers, is
on the corner of Adam Street and has been built in a typical
'Adam style' to blend in with the Adelphi.

Nos 47, 48 and 49

Even older buildings are hidden behind shop fronts in the
drawing (*opp. top left*); at No 48, Jenkins the Printseller, may
have a Regency shop but the building is probably Jacobean.
Next door at No 49 is the famous name of Bewlay the
Tobacconist.

Nos 174, 175

No 174 (*opp. top right*) with its distinctive projecting storey
might be Elizabethan behind its sash windows and stucco.
By contrast, the eighteenth-century building next door has
a modern neo-classical shop front which, according to
Scharf's note, is in white marble with brass window sashes.

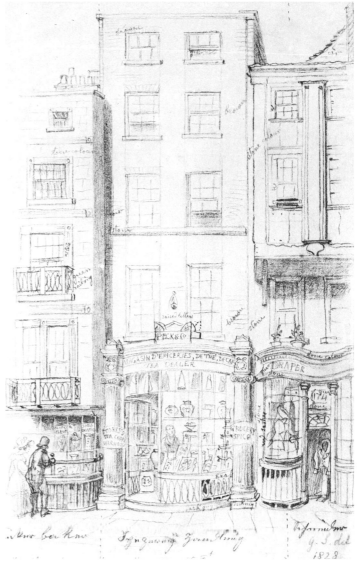

No 83, Cock & Bottle

This sign, once very common, indicates that the pub sells beer on draught or in bottle, cock being an archaic word for the spigot or tap in a barrel. The grapes show that it also sells wine.

This typical eighteenth-century tavern (*right*) was modernised some time before 1838 and became a wine and spirit merchants in the 1890s.

It was demolished in 1899 when the Strand was widened and the Hotel Cecil extended its frontage to cover the site.

STRAND : North Side

The Strand was not as fashionable a thoroughfare as Regent Street, Piccadilly or Bond Street but what it lacked in elegance it made up for in variety, not only in the extraordinary array of commodities for sale but in the ever-changing assortment of shop-fronts to attract the eye. Numbers 470–480 in the drawing *above* were all demolished in the 1830s to clear the way for the improvements south of St Martin-in-the-Fields and Scharf hastened to record them before they went. The gap in the middle is Lancaster Court which led straight up to St Martin's Church. To the far right is No 470, the Hungerford Coffee House, named after Hungerford Market which it faced across the road (see p. 58). Though it is first mentioned in the Vestry minutes of St Martin's in 1790 its handsome façade with its carved swags and small-paned windows suggest a date around the 1750s. It was noted for its file of old newspapers and at this time (1829) the proprietor was Lydia Tart. Next door is William Stretton, Furnishing Ironmonger, and then William Pocknell's Barrel'd Oyster and Shellfish Warehouse where you could eat on the premises or take away.

Pocknell's Establishment

Pocknell's establishment is seen in greater detail in this separate drawing (*left*) which gives a rare view of the inside of the shop looking through to the dining area at the back and to the stairs leading to the living accommodation.

John Gardner's Shop

Number 484 was the shop (*below*) of John Gardner, Lamp Manufacturer and Oil Man. Scharf gives us an invaluable record of how the oil was delivered by being pumped into the shop, and captures the moment when an unfortunate lady experiences the hazard of walking under the leaky oil pipe.

STRAND : North Side

Scharf made many drawings of this part of the north side of the Strand from No 454, just opposite Villiers Street, eastward to Castle Court (to the far right of the picture *above*). In the 1830s, all these buildings were replaced in the West Strand Improvements by the triangular block which still exists today and includes the rebuilt Coutts's Bank with its 'pepper-pots'. In the centre, a fireman is rolling up a hose after the fire which is seen in more detail in the lower watercolour. The fire started at five o'clock on the morning of 5 September 1824 in the shop of Mr Martin, a sausage-maker, and spread next door to Mr Hatfield's, the porkman. These houses with projecting bays were of some antiquity and timber framed, a fact commented upon by *The Times* (6 September 1824) in its account of the fire: 'The houses being built of wood, fears were entertained for the safety of the Bunch of Grapes public house – and the house next to Mr Hatfield's – as they were also of wood as well as old and new Round Courts close behind of similar materials.' In 1843 Scharf tried to sell his painting of the fire to the Phoenix Fire Office without success; hardly surprising since the engine which put out the fire was a Sun Fire Office machine.

STRAND : North Side

The flamboyant building (*above*) jutting out into the Strand is Exeter Change just before it was demolished to widen the road. It stood on the north side and was built about 1676 on the site of Exeter House after which it was named. For the convenience of pedestrians a footpath ran right through the middle of it. On either side were small booths and shops selling all manner of goods making this London's first shopping arcade. The upper floor was put to an extraordinary variety of uses. In the eighteenth century it had been a funeral parlour where the corpses of distinguished persons lay in state to be viewed by a curious public. It had been used for lectures and exhibitions of all kinds. At one time it was an auction room and, as the Patagonian Theatre, it was a puppet playhouse, but towards the end of its existence it achieved its greatest fame as a menagerie. Apart from the small collection at the Tower there was nowhere else to see wild animals and with its lions and tigers and monkeys and, above all, 'Chunee' its famous elephant, it became one of the sights of London. 'Chunee', especially after his stage appearance in a Covent Garden pantomime, was as beloved as 'Jumbo' was to be by a later generation, and 'Chunee' caused a sensation when, in 1826, he became unmanageable and had to be shot. Exeter Change was closed on 18 April 1829 and sold by auction four days later, though it would appear that the passageway through the arcade was still open in June when Scharf made his drawing. On the extreme right is the pit entrance to the Lyceum Theatre and on the left, Wellington Street leads to Waterloo Bridge.

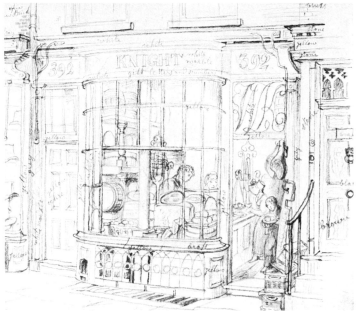

No 392

At No 392 (*above*) was the charming shop of William Knight whose initials in wrought iron make up the fanlight. The window has a novel feature: a section can be removed to give an unimpeded view of his display of hams and cheeses.

No 238

A complete contrast was the fish shop (*above*) at the extreme north-east end of the Strand hard against Temple Bar which eschewed such refinements as windows. Known as the 'Old Bulk Shop' (bulk meaning stall in front of a shop) it claimed to go back to the time of Henry VIII though this was probably taking its undoubted antiquity too far. Here in 1775 was born William Crockford and here he made enough money to enable him to establish the famous gambling club which bore his name. He would never allow the shop to be altered in his lifetime; he died in 1844 and the ancient shop was demolished two years later.

No 244

The entire frontage of No 244 (*above*) was an advertisement for Lardner's Blacking Manufactory. Modelled in plaster on either side of the windows were a pair of Hessian boots, oriental slippers, and inverted blacking bottles over boot jacks.

in the Strand — near Temple Bar   London J. S.

PICKETT STREET

Robinson's Eating House was on the north side of the Strand ten doors west of Temple Bar and next to the entrance to Ship Yard. It was No 247 Strand, but it was also No 2 Pickett Street, which must have confused Scharf who did not identify it. It was part of one of London's earliest improvement schemes, the brainchild of Alderman William Pickett, a silversmith of Bond Street. For years he had campaigned to have that part of the Strand which entered the City tidied up and made worthy of its importance. It is difficult to visualise how very cluttered it was. The church of St Clement Danes was hemmed in on all sides so closely that the passageway on the south was no more than 30 ft wide while the northern gap was a mere 5 ft at its narrowest point and impossible for traffic. Worst of all, between St Clement Danes and Temple Bar was a long wedge of ramshackle buildings, many dating from before the Great Fire, backing on to an ancient thoroughfare called Butcher Row.

Just before his death in 1796, Alderman Pickett succeeded in having an Act of Parliament passed: 'for Widening and Improving the Entrance to the City of London near Temple Bar', which resulted in the Butcher Row block and all the houses surrounding St Clement Danes being demolished. Malcolm in his *Anecdotes of London* observed: 'A stranger who had visited London in 1790 would, on his return in 1804, be astonished to find a spacious area, with the church nearly in the centre, on the site of Butcher Row.'

The Strand, widened to 135 ft, now encircled St Clement Danes with a quadrant of elegant houses and shops. (Owing to their high cost and the difficulty of selling them, they had to be given away as prizes in a lottery.) The whole scheme was finished by 1811 and the new section of the Strand between Nos 245 and 265 was named Pickett Street with its own numbering. The name never did catch on, however, and after some years it was dropped and the new houses became part of the Strand. The whole site was cleared in the 1870s to make way for the Law Courts.

near the New Post Office site

4

ROAD UP

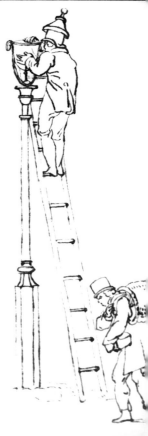

GAS MAINS

When George Scharf came to London in 1816 its streets were still lit mainly by oil lamps although gas lighting had been introduced nearly ten years earlier. In 1818 he observed the lamplighter (*left*) who had put the lid from the lamp on his hat so that he had both hands free to tend the oil and wick.

It took the public some time to overcome its fears of explosion and asphyxiation but by 1825, when the watercolour *above* was painted, gas was beginning to be accepted, not only for street lighting but in private homes. 'I have it in every part of my house to the entire exclusion of tallow and oil,' wrote a correspondent in the *Sun* for 13 May 1823, 'my chamber and nursery having the light burning regularly through the whole night.' Gas was supplied to individual houses through the narrow, straight pipes clearly seen in Scharf's painting branching out at right angles from the largest of the three parallel pipes suspended over the sewer excavation. The other two convey water.

By 1834, the date of the drawing *far left*, Leigh's *New Picture of London* was able to say 'Nearly all the streets are lighted by gas, an improvement which has only been introduced within a few years.' Once gas became accepted its use developed rapidly and by 1842 the whole of the metropolis was gas-lit, consuming nearly nine million cubic feet of gas every 24 hours.

Charles Knight in his *London*, published at this time, gives a vivid impression of what this transformation must have looked like to someone brought up in a London poorly lit by oil and candle: 'The noblest prospect in the world is London from Hampstead Heath on a bright winter's evening. The stars are shining in heaven, but there are thousands of earthly stars glittering in the city there spread before us: and we can see the dim shapes of mighty buildings afar off, showing their dark masses amidst the glowing atmosphere that hangs over the capital for miles.'

Street shored up for a Sewer
G.S. Septbr 1841

SEWERS

The report of the Metropolitan Sanitary Commission of 1848 set in motion a programme of reform in London's drainage which was to culminate some 20 years later in Sir Joseph Bazalgette's great interceptory sewer system which is still in use today. But the sewers on which the Commissioners reported were those which George Scharf was drawing in the 1840s. They were antiquated, in poor condition, in constant need of repair and discharged their sewage into the Thames. The drawing *above*, dated 1841, shows the shoring up of the houses in Paul Street, near Moorgate, to prevent their collapse while a sewer is being dug. It will join the existing sewer running at right angles to it in Worship Street seen (*right*) being enlarged. On the *far right* can be seen the sewers in Bloomsbury Street in 1845; their improved design, introduced by Holborn's sanitary engineer John Roe, was highly commended by the Commissioners.

PRINTSELLER

wood

Stones

wood

earth

wood

rough brick wall

door

earth

upright
Earth and a
few Bricks

a mound of Earth

73

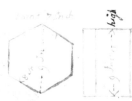

ying down a ____ _____ _____ _____ _____

____der pavement for

____, but did not answear.

This in Oxford Street
about the same time

G. Scharf

d's

____ the Strand 23 May 1840. ____ ____ ____ ____ description of the Asphalt page 90 Coppy Book

74

WOODEN PAVING

The constant roar of London traffic 'as if all the noises of all the wheels of all the carriages in creation were mingled and ground together into one subdued, hoarse, moaning hum' (Masson, *Memories, of London in the 'Forties*) was due, not only to the clatter of horses' hooves, but the rumble of iron-shod wheels on uneven paving. Traffic grew to such proportions and the problem of noise so acute that it became a matter of some municipal concern and, in the 1830s, experiments were made to find the ideal paving material. In 1839 a stretch of just under 150 yds of Oxford Street between Tottenham Court Road/Charles Street (the turning which led to Soho Square) was laid with no fewer than twelve different specimens of pavement consisting of combinations of bitumen, stone, asphalt, granite and wood. It was the wood which, according to the *Gentleman's Magazine* in Feb. 1839, drew the most attention: 'the noiseless tendency of which made the vehicles passing along appear to be rolling over a thick carpet or rug'. It was so successful that wood was chosen to pave the whole of Oxford Street and after it had been down

for six months the *Gentleman's Magazine* in April 1840 reported that 7000 vehicles and 12,000 horses had passed over it 'with scarcely any sign of wear'.

Top left   As might be expected, George Scharf was on hand to record the work of the paviors as they laid the experimental paving in Oxford Street.

Left   After the success of the Oxford Street experiment, wood paving was used all over London. Here Staed's patent blocks, the same as used in Oxford Street, are being laid in the Strand.

Above   Another paving contractor, Mr Mortimer of 2 Frith Street, Soho, commissioned Scharf to make this lithograph of his patent wood pavement being laid in front of St Martin-in-the-Fields in 1842. The work took him 111 hours for which he charged £5. 'If Mr Mortimer buys many prints, I shall get more' Scharf noted in his journal.

WATER CARTS

Water carts (*above*), used to wash down the roads, were a common sight in the more affluent parts of town. The carts were usually horse-drawn; these, pictured in Bloomsbury Square in 1828, were pulled by a four-man team. Alfred Rosling Bennett, writing in the 1920s, recalled the water carts of his early childhood: 'they were filled from road-side pumps instead of hydrants, which involved much pumping by the men and, as a consequence, a great deal of bad language. The pumps, six feet high, had spouts above the level of the carts, into which water was conducted by movable troughs.'

ROAD SWEEPERS

These road sweepers (*left*), as distinct from the ubiquitous crossing-sweepers who only cleared pathways through mud and snow for individuals in the hope of receiving tips, were employed by cleaning contractors to sweep up the mud created by the water carts. This was then shovelled up and carted away to be sold by the contractor for the fertilising properties of the manure it contained. The street-sweeping machine, which was invented about 1845, did not entirely put these men out of work. The machine was efficient only on a level surface and the sweepers were still needed to get into awkward places, and what they called 'nicks and holes'.

5

COVENT GARDEN

Eine Irländische
Gemüs händlerin.
Une marchande de
l'egume Irlandoise.

Kinder aus den Frey Schulten,
nach altem Costume gekleidet.
Enfans de charité.

Ein Matrose.
Un Matelot.

Ein Bauer.
Un Paysan.

Ein Berg Schotte.
Un Ecossois.

Ein Feuer Man.
Un Pompier.

Ein Kohlenträger.
Un Charbonnier.

COVENT GARDEN HUSTINGS

Polling for the two Members of Parliament for Westminster had taken place at the hustings erected in front of St Paul's Church, Covent Garden, since at least 1701 and was to continue until 1868, the last general election before the introduction of the secret ballot in 1872.

They were lively events, sometimes riotous, always noisy, and this one, brought about by the dissolution of Parliament on 10 June 1818 after a sitting of five and a half years, was no exception.

Unlike the political cartoonists of the time, Scharf shows no interest in the outcome of the election. The hustings, the large temporary wooden shed from which the candidates address the crowd, is pushed into the background and he uses the event merely as an excuse for depicting (*left*) one of his favourite subjects, the workaday people of London's streets.

In spite of this preoccupation, however, Scharf's eye for detail records on posters the names of candidates, and a placard announcing the state of the poll on the 15th shows Romilly and Burdett leading the field ahead of Maxwell and Hunt. The election was in fact won by Sir Francis Burdett and by Sir Samuel Romilly, who lived only a few weeks to enjoy his seat in Parliament.

The Parliamentary session was also short-lived, for eighteen months later George III died and Parliament was dissolved. A new election was held and with uncharacteristic business acumen Scharf re-published his old print by merely altering the date and a few names.

Below left The key to the market figures, identified in French and German, issued with the print.

Below After the 1818 election, Sir Francis Burdett's supporters celebrate in the Strand.

Milch Mädchen.   Eine Irländerin.   Ein Träger.
Une Laitière.   Une Irlandoise.   Un Porteur.

COVENT GARDEN MARKET
North Side looking West

Street traders began selling their wares in the open piazza
of Covent Garden soon after it was created as part of the
Bedford Estate development in the reign of Charles I. But
not being legally recognised as a market, the Bedfords derived
no revenue from it. This was rectified by the fifth Earl, who,
in 1670, was granted a Royal charter authorising him and his
heirs to hold a market 'for the buying and selling of all manner
of fruits, flowers, roots and herbs'. From then on, being able
to charge rents and tolls, he encouraged the growth of the
market. At first the traders were allowed to set up their stalls
only on the south side of the piazza. However, throughout
the eighteenth century the market grew rapidly and by 1825,
when Scharf painted the watercolour (*see previous page*), it had
spread over the whole area of the square. As if to underline
the original intention, the Bedford Estate built some permanent market buildings on the south side but little effort was
made to control the haphazard erection of wooden sheds and
stalls elsewhere as long as the rents were paid. It is this lively
area of the market, the north side looking west, which cap-
tivated Scharf. These wooden, lead-roofed sheds, have no
provision for locking goods away; they are merely shelters
from the rain under which traders could sell fruit and vegetables brought in from the surrounding countryside.

East End of the Market (*above left & right*)

These two drawings form a continuous view looking east
towards Russell Street. On the left is the Piazza Hotel. It
was here in 1809 that Richard Brinsley Sheridan, bottle in
hand and watching the burning of Drury Lane Theatre put
an end to his income and his career, quipped, 'Cannot a man
take a glass of wine by his own fireside?' The Hotel was
demolished in 1858 and the Floral Hall erected on its site.
At right angles, running south to the corner of Russell Street,
is the Bedford Hotel, demolished in 1888. Over the rooftops
can be seen the Theatre Royal, Covent Garden, designed by
Robert Smirke and opened on 18 September 1809. On its
roof a trumpet-blowing figure serves as a wind-vane for the
ventilation funnel. Gas lighting had been introduced into the
auditorium in 1817 and the enormous chandelier which hung
from the centre of the ceiling made the extraction of the fumes
a prime consideration. The theatre made its own gas but when
on 18 November 1828, just five months after this drawing
was made, the gasometer blew up killing three people, the
management announced in the playbills that henceforth
candles and oil would be used.

Right A typical market stall

G Scharf del 1818   in Coventgarden Market

COVENT GARDEN MARKET
Lock-up Shops

The Duke of Bedford first erected permanent shops on the south side of the piazza as early as 1705 and they were rebuilt in 1748. These small lock-up shops, 106 of them, were built in two rows of long, single-storey blocks with low-pitched lead roofs from which chimneys projected. The block *above left* shows the south-east corner where the communal market scales stand for weighing potatoes which were always sold at the south side. On the right of the picture we can see the corner of Carpenter's Coffee House which is shown in the drawing on the *left*.

There was a Carpenter's Coffee House here prior to 1768 but this one, probably only a revival of the old name, first appeared in the directories in 1809 when the proprietor was Robert Way. When Scharf drew it twenty years later it was still in the same family.

The view *above* is looking west down the middle of the market towards the portico of St Paul's Church. The row of permanent shops contrasts strongly with the muddle of sheds which cluttered up the rest of the piazza.

On the *right* is the western end of the same southern block seen *top left*. Probably drawn on a Sunday when there was no trading, it shows the empty open 'shop' where goods were normally exposed. James Butler, Herbalist and Seedsman, who appears to be under Royal patronage, remained on the same site after the new market had been built. Indeed there was a Butler here until the end of the 1890s.

View taken in front of Covent Garden Church, May

COVENT GARDEN: New Market

Covent Garden was not the only fruit and vegetable market in London but it was the greatest, and as far as the growers were concerned, all roads led to 'the Garden'. It had always been relatively easy for produce to reach the market from the growers on the northern outskirts of London, but the opening of Waterloo Bridge in 1817 added enormously to the influx by giving direct access to the hundreds of market gardens of Kent and Surrey. The carts, so well observed in the drawing *below left*, were loaded at sunset and by one o'clock in the morning they had set out, filling the roads around London throughout the night, with the aim of reaching the market by about four o'clock when the dealers arrived. The congestion of the roads in the early hours was no great problem but the concentration of carts and wagons once they reached Covent Garden became intolerable. Moreover the market attracted dealers in all sorts of miscellaneous goods who occupied the centre of the piazza so that the surrounding roadways became cluttered with the stalls and baskets of those who could find no place in the market itself. As the market continued to spread, something had to be done to regulate and control its growth. In 1826 an Act had authorised the purchase of some land owned by the Duke of Bedford for the widening of the Strand. The Duke sold this property for £29,000 and devoted the money to the erection of a permanent market.

The architect he chose was Charles Fowler. His design, in Graeco-Roman style, provided for three parallel ranges of buildings containing shops, offices and cellars. In addition, the pitching of stalls in various parts of the market outside the building was strictly regulated with the scale of rents to be charged for each type of stand precisely laid down. Building began in September 1828 and on the *right* can be seen the progress made by August the following year. The view is of the southern range where one of the grey granite columns of the Tuscan colonnade is being hoisted into position.

Below right we have the view (in May 1829) looking due west with the northern range completed. It shows one of the square pavilions which still stands at each of the four corners. Fowler wanted round-headed windows here, but the Duke changed them to square, which shows the personal interest he took in the design. By May 1830 the new Covent Garden Market was complete looking, at least as far as the outside perimeter is concerned, very much as the restored market looks today.

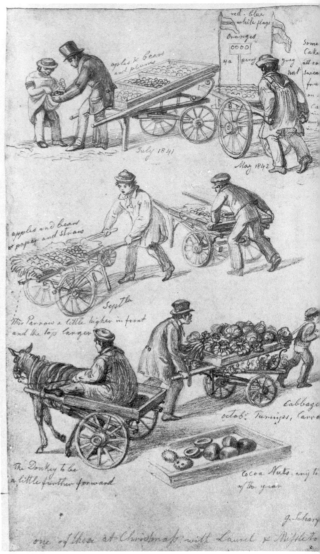

DICKENS IN THE 'GARDEN'

Once the agents of the hotels and restaurants had bought the pick of the crops and the choicest of fruit, the surplus was sold off more cheaply to the itinerant traders. It was then that the costermongers moved in with their hand-carts and donkey barrows. Charles Dickens observed the scene in *Sketches by Boz* a few years after the new market was opened:

'Covent Garden market, and the avenues leading to it, are thronged with carts of all sorts, sizes, and descriptions, from the heavy lumbering wagon, with its four stout horses, to the jingling costermonger's cart, with its consumptive donkey. The pavement is already strewed with decayed cabbage-leaves, broken hay-bands, and all the indescribable litter of a vegetable market; men are shouting, carts backing, horses neighing, boys fighting, basket-women talking, piemen expatiating on the excellence of their pastry, and donkeys braying.'

6

ART, SCIENCE
& LEISURE

KING'S COLLEGE, STRAND

(*Previous page*) The lecture theatre in 1831, the year the College was opened on the east side of new Somerset House. Preparations are being made for a lecture in geology possibly to be given by Charles Lyell, the new foundation's Professor of Geology.

ROYAL ACADEMY, Somerset House

The Royal Academy was closely linked with Somerset House
from its early days, for though its first exhibitions were held
in a house in Pall Mall, in 1771 it was allowed to use rooms
in the old Tudor palace for its Library and Drawing School.
When the new Somerset House was built the Royal Academy
was allocated the whole of the ground and upper floors on
the right of the entrance gateway from the Strand. As soon
as the block was ready for occupation, George III comman-
ded that an exhibition should be held, and on 28 April 1780
he was given a preview of the show and a conducted tour
by Sir Joshua Reynolds, the founder President. It was opened
to the public on 1 May.

Scharf's watercolour (*left*) shows the entrance hall, full of
classical statuary. On the right, the porter sits in front of his
lodge; the other door leads to the Life School. Beyond the
columned screen, where stands a copy of the Farnese
Hercules, is the elliptical stairway leading to the exhibition
gallery which extended over the northern half of the entrance
gateway. It was up these steep winding stairs that all works
submitted for exhibition (and these were the days of huge,
heavily framed canvases) had to be hauled by ropes.

Scharf's painting was made in 1836, the last year that the
annual exhibition was held at Somerset House. The Royal
Academy then moved to the newly built National Gallery and
in 1868 found its final home at Burlington House.

CHANTREY'S FOUNDRY

The foundry (*right*) of the sculptor Sir Francis Chantrey in
Eccleston Place, Pimlico, shows the statues of George IV on
the left and William Pitt on the right. Pitt was erected in
Hanover Square at a cost of £7000 and was unveiled on 22
August 1831.

WATER COLOUR SOCIETY

Watercolourists, once regarded as the poor relations of the oil-painters, had already achieved a status of respectability by the time George Scharf had arrived in London. Ever since the mid eighteenth century their work had been accepted for exhibitions but it was always in competition with oils. In the Royal Academy it was not even considered worthy enough to be shown in the Great Gallery at Somerset House and was relegated to small rooms among the inferior oils. Moreover, watercolourists were sacrificing the delicacy and freshness of their medium by painting heavily in a competitive attempt to emulate the richness of oil painting.

It was an intolerable position and in 1805 sixteen artists got together to form the Society of Painters in Water Colours. They held their first exhibition (the first devoted to the medium) at 20 Lower Brook Street and it opened in April 1805.

The success of this and subsequent exhibitions led to the formation of a rival society, the Associated Artists in Water Colours, in 1808 but this broke up four years later. However, it was revived in 1832 as the New Society of Painters in Water Colours and it was this society that George Scharf joined. He exhibited one painting, *View of the Ladies' Bazaar*, at their first show. In 1833 he was a member of the Committee and in 1834 he was on the Committee of Management.

Scharf's painting (*right*) shows the third exhibition in 1834 held at No 16 Old Bond Street, a marvellous evocation of a typical art gallery of the time. Though the watercolourists had long enjoyed their independence they continued to mount their pictures in heavy gilt frames as if they were still competing with oil paintings and cram them together just as they had been at the Royal Academy. Dominating the gallery is 'The Screen' on which they have managed to hang no fewer than 87 paintings, 42 on the side we can see, 45 on the other. Showing great restraint, Scharf has chosen a viewpoint which does not include his own painting, No 114 in the catalogue, *Old and New London Bridges as they appeared in December 1831*.

The Society's next exhibition was held at Exeter Hall in the Strand, and Scharf had six paintings hanging including the originals for some of his Zoo lithographs, his *Panoramic View of the Ruins of St Stephen's* and the painting he did the previous year of the Old Bond Street Gallery.

In 1836 he resigned his membership 'in consequence', he wrote in his journal for 21 July, 'of my being unable to continue paying the subscription of 6 shillings per month and felt it very hard to have to pay a fine of 5 shillings each time when I was a month behind paying it'.

2979.76   G. Scharf Pinx. 1834

93

SCIENCE FOR THE MASSES

In the 1830s the public began to take an interest in technology and applied science, stimulated by the publication of popular journals such as the *Mirror* and the *Penny Magazine*. These were illustrated with wood engravings which intrigued the ordinary reader but did little to satisfy his curiosity. What was needed was some institution where the new scientific marvels could be exhibited and lectures and demonstrations could be given. This need was met by the opening, in 1832, of the Gallery of Practical Science, later to be known as the Adelaide Gallery, in the triangular block which Nash had just built on the north side of the Strand. Apart from the 'pepper-pots' on its corners, which are still there, the most arresting feature of this new block was the Lowther Arcade, a shop-lined passage running from the Strand to Adelaide Street, later to be replaced by Coutts's Bank. The Adelaide Gallery was to the north of the Lowther Arcade, running parallel to it, with an entrance at No 7 Adelaide Street and another from the arcade itself. The gallery had only just opened when Scharf made his drawing (*right*) and did not yet exhibit many of the wonders with which it was soon to dazzle the public. The drawing does, however, already show its two most popular attractions. Down the middle of the gallery is the 100 ft long canal containing 6000 gallons of water on which clockwork paddle-boats ply, and on the right, actually being demonstrated, is Perkins's steam-operated machine gun. This could fire bullets at the rate of 20 per second; and the bullets, on reaching the cast-iron target, seen at the end of the gallery 100 ft away, were flattened to the thickness of tin-foil.

POLYTECHNIC INSTITUTION

The Adelaide Gallery's great rival was the Polytechnic Institution, opened on 6 August 1838 at No 309 Regent Street where it still stands today though rebuilt. Originally called the Royal Gallery of Arts and Sciences, it received a Royal charter in 1839 and was dedicated to the encouragement of inventors who were given free space in which to exhibit their machines and models. But its function was primarily to instruct and educate the public in an appreciation of practical science and mechanics by offering a set programme of lectures and demonstrations. It also had to pay its way and admission, as with the Adelaide Gallery, was a shilling. The resemblance did not end there and Scharf's lithograph (*left*), made in 1840, shows how similar the two exhibitions were. But everything was bigger and better at the Polytechnic. It covered a far larger area with several lecture rooms and demonstration theatres in addition to the galleried Great Hall, 120 ft long and 40 ft wide. Whereas the Adelaide had one miniature canal for the display of its model boats the Polytechnic had two

holding 10,000 gallons of water with lock-gates and water-wheels. The Adelaide had a small glass diving-bell occupied by a mouse; the Polytechnic had a huge iron one occupied by six human divers. This can be seen at the rear of the hall. Made of cast iron with thick plate-glass windows, it weighed 3 tons, was 5 ft high and 4 ft 8 in. in diameter at the mouth.

Around the inside was seating for six people at a time who paid a shilling each for the privilege of being submerged in the water tank at the end of the canal into which the bell was lowered from a massive swing crane. It had its most distinguished customer in 1840 if we are to believe 'Our Weekly Gossip' column in the *Athenaeum* for 12 December. It refers to 'the diving bell (in which, by the way, HRH The Prince Albert lately descended)'. A Royal adventure which *The Times* correspondent, who reported the Prince's visit, did not see fit to mention.

BRITISH MUSEUM

George Scharf knew the British Museum well. In the days before its natural history exhibits were moved to South Kensington he was employed drawing fossils and colouring casts of bones, while his eldest son George was to achieve some importance as official draughtsman at several of the Museum's archaeological expeditions. Although he lived to see the British Museum as we now know it, he was most familiar with its original home, Montague House.

The 'father' of the British Museum, Sir Hans Sloane, died in 1753 bequeathing his curiosities to the nation for the payment of £20,000 to his two daughters. In order to raise the money, a public lottery was organised which brought in £300,000. After paying out £200,000 in prize money, there was enough left over to pay, not only for Sloane's collection, but two other great collections – the Cotton Library and the Harleian Manuscripts – and to purchase a suitable building in which to house them. The Trustees bought, for a mere £10,000, Montague House, a French-style seventeenth-century mansion with 7½ acres of garden behind it allowing for expansion. It was opened to the public, with admission by ticket, on 15 January 1759.

Great Russell Street

The south-west approach to Montague House in the 1840s (*above*), looking east along Great Russell Street. Montague House lay farther north out of the picture on exactly the site of the present building. What appears above is actually the back of the west wing of the quadrangle.

Old Entrance

Farther along Great Russell Street was the highly decorative gateway to the courtyard (*top right*) just about to be demolished in 1850. The Grenadier Guardsmen on duty outside are the picket with which the Museum was provided up to 1863 when the practice was discontinued.

Courtyard

Once through the grand entrance the visitor found himself in this spacious courtyard (*right*). The great gate was in the middle of an Ionic colonnade; opposite was the old mansion while to left and right were the wings occupied by Museum staff. This is the site of today's forecourt.

Museum Entrance

We get some idea of the magnificence of Montague House from this watercolour (*above*) of the entrance hall painted in August 1845 just before its demolition. The statues are those of Sir Joseph Banks, the naturalist, by Chantrey and, on the right, Roubiliac's famous Shakespeare which can now be seen in the King's Library.

One of the 'studious and curious persons' whom the original Act of Parliament directed the Museum to admit, is signing the visitors' book (the only requirement after the abolition of tickets in 1805) watched by the Head Porter, Mr Bishop. Three other porters are dressed in their 'Windsor Livery' of blue coat with scarlet collar and cuffs. They are identified by George Scharf in his journal as 'Monticelli, Bayard and Hind'. At the door stands a policeman in top hat, 'Mr Neal, 149 A Division'. He was the constable who took in charge William Lloyd, the man who smashed the Portland Vase a few months before this watercolour was painted.

Giraffe Staircase

Had our visitor turned left he would have mounted a staircase (*top right*) cluttered with stuffed animals to be confronted on the upper landing by a rhinoceros and three huge giraffes. Although the first live giraffe to be seen in England was one given to George IV in 1827, two of these stuffed examples were here before then. A German visitor, Prince Puckler-Muskau, mentions in his *English Diary* under 15 October 1826 that at the top of the stairs were 'two enormous giraffes, in the character of stuffed guards, or emblems of English taste'.

The Zoological Department, with its 'stuffed tigers and medicated bird skins', was transferred in 1883 to the Natural History Museum, South Kensington.

Sculpture Gallery

From its foundation the Museum's collections grew rapidly and old Montague House was soon filled to bursting point. Wooden sheds had been erected in the garden to house the overflow, and with the addition of Sir William Hamilton's classical sculptures and an influx of Egyptian antiquities captured from the French in 1802, serious thought was given to building new galleries.

The first was erected at the north-west corner of Montague House extending northwards along the west side of the garden. The Sculpture Gallery, as it was called, was opened on 3 July 1808 by Queen Charlotte. Here (*right*) we see it in 1827 looking through to the Townley Gallery which was added to the original plans to accommodate the superb collection of Greek and Roman antiquities formed by Charles Townley, a Museum Trustee. Included among the wonderful sculptures was the famous *Discobolus* or discus-thrower which can be faintly seen at the end of the gallery.

THE NEW BRITISH MUSEUM

As the Museum continued to grow, a programme of building expansion was planned by the architect, Robert Smirke. The first part of the scheme was the erection of two parallel wings on either side of the garden to the north of Montague House. This drawing (*above*), dated July 1828, shows the building activity in the garden. Joining at right angles the north-west corner of Montague House on the left is the Sculpture Gallery leading to the Townley Gallery the interior of which is seen on the previous page. North of this is part of Smirke's new building. He had just finished the new wing on the east side to house the 'King's Library', a collection of 65,250 volumes and 19,000 unbound tracts amassed by George III. This was the first completed section of the Museum building we know today. The west wing *above* could not be completed until the Townley Gallery was demolished in 1846. Later this garden was the site of the great Reading Room.

More Expansion

In 1842, the antiquities discovered by Charles Fellows in Lycia, in Asia Minor, began arriving, the Admiralty having mounted an expedition to retrieve them. The 'Lycian Marbles' were of such interest that a special gallery was built for them and here (*top right*) we see its foundations being laid in 1845 on the west side and parallel with the front of the new museum. The view is looking south across Great Russell Street, where some of the new houses have yet to be built, to the steeple of St George's, Bloomsbury.

Scharf's interest in the details of building activity is evident in the two drawings he made in 1845, of the work on the site of the Lycian Room (*right*) and the masons shaping the Portland stone columns for the colonnade (*left*).

PLEASURE BOATS

'Sketch taken on Board a Steam Boat going to Gravesend 7 Sept. 1842' is George Scharf's caption to the drawing (*left*).

It is the *Eagle* which left from the pier at Hungerford Market for Gravesend at 9 a.m. calling at Swan Stairs, London Bridge (*above*), a quarter of an hour later, to pick up more passengers. She returned at 4.30 p.m. and the fare for the 31 miles each way was 1s and 1s 6d on Sundays. The *Eagle* was probably built on the Clyde about 1819 and was, like all steamboats of the period, paddle-driven. The casing for the paddle-wheels can be seen on either side of the boat in Scharf's drawing looking towards the stern. On the left is the tiny kitchen supplying refreshments. The little orchestra was a regular feature which went back to the early 1800s when the steamboat was first introduced and proved to be a serious rival to the long-established sailing hoys working the 'long ferry' as the journey between London and Gravesend was called. They did all they could to discredit the new-fangled means of transport, and the steamboat people

countered by offering to provide playing cards and draughtboards and a band of music for entertainment. It became a regular practice, though by Scharf's time they had ceased to be paid by the proprietors who merely allowed them to travel free and pass round the hat for gratuities.

SWAN STAIRS

A celebrated landing-place (*above*) on the north bank of the river just west of London Bridge, named after an ancient tavern in Thames Street. In the days when the tide rushed through the narrow arches of London Bridge with such ferocity that any traveller foolish enough to be rowed through these rapids risked death by drowning, it was customary to land here, walk round the Bridge to Billingsgate and, assuming that the waterman had survived 'shooting the bridge', pick up the boat again.

COACHES AND HORSES

Scharf lived through the golden age of coaching, the days when every inn had some sort of coach-yard behind it, when every landlord's livelihood depended on the housing and care of horses. Even small pubs such as the Black Bull and the Red Lion in Grays Inn Lane (*left*) have an archway between them leading to a world of horses where, as the notices outside tell us, can be found a forge, a veterinary surgeon, a coach and cart wheelwright and a livery stable. Over the rooftops can be seen Meux's Brewery, later to become Reid's.

Castle and Falcon *(below left)*

A typical coaching inn standing on the east side of Aldersgate Street nearly opposite the church of St Botolph. It was just one of over a dozen inns lining the street which was the principal entrance into the City from the north. Stage-coaches could be boarded here for Leeds or Birmingham and, according to the notice at the end of the yard, 'goods conveyed to any part of the Kingdom'. It managed to survive the collapse of the coaching boom by becoming a railway booking office and remained here until about 1900.

Livery Stables *(below)*

In 1827 when Scharf made this drawing, the omnibus was two years in the future, and there were over 450 livery stables in London for the convenience of those not rich enough to have a carriage of their own and who did not choose to travel around town in the primitive cabs of the time. Here they could hire a horse or keep one of their own and have it fed and groomed for a fixed charge. Cotterell's Livery Stable was on the north side of Compton Street, Bloomsbury, next door to George Hughes' Printing Office. Though Compton Street has been largely rebuilt and is now part of Tavistock Place, the archway leading to the mews still exists.

Castle and Falcon, General Coach and Waggon Office, Aldersgate Street, May 18

Stage-Coach *(above)*

This lively drawing was made in 1829 just before the railway put an end to the coaching era. As it shows the Exeter coach in Piccadilly it must be setting out from either Hatchett's White Horse Cellar or the Gloucester Coffee House which were the two termini for the West Country route. They were also the starting points for Royal Mail coaches which, for convenience, picked up their letter-bags here instead of at the General Post Office.

Steam Carriage *(below)*

A pioneer attempt to replace the horse was made by Goldsworthy Gurney who invented the steam carriage. Big enough to carry eighteen people and travel at a speed of 15 mph, it was the first self-propelling or motor coach to carry fare-paying passengers. Scharf made this drawing in 1827, the year it was first seen in London's streets. A few years later Gurney improved the design, but gave up his experiments in 1831.

ZOO VIEWS

Ever since 1826 when the Zoological Society was first granted a plot of land in Regent's Park it had grown and expanded rapidly. George Scharf watched this development and the building of the various houses to accommodate the animals and birds with an artist's eye and a sketch-book.

By 1835 he had made a set of lithographic views which he took to the headquarters of the Society at 33 Bruton Street to obtain the Council's permission to sell them in the gardens. He was no stranger to the Fellows. For some years he had been making drawings for them some of which appeared as lithographs in the first volume of the Society's *Transactions* which were published in this same year. They approved of his *Views* and on 21 June he delivered a consignment personally. They were a great success even with the press. A typical review appeared in the *Morning Advertiser* for 23 December 1835: 'It is impossible for anyone to look at these views for a moment, without recognising in them the hand of the master. They are not only faithful copies from nature, of the subjects they represent, but they are beautiful specimens of art, executed with skill, and displaying a purity of taste but rarely to be met with.'

Bear Pit

Just by the Bear Pit (*above*) was a little rustic shop 'for the sale of cakes, fruit, nuts and other articles which the visitors may be disposed to give to the different animals'. Feeding of animals by the public (totally forbidden since 1968) was actively encouraged in these early days even to the provision of a long stick with which to feed buns to the bears. This was one of the prime attractions of the Zoo to judge from this passage from *The Public Buildings of Westminster Described*, published by John Harris in 1831: 'Within a large bricked area, dug many feet below the surface of the ground, and well protected by high railings, some Bears may be seen. Their character may be somewhat studied by exciting their jealousy and ferocity, which the bystanders abundantly do, by giving them cakes at the end of a long pole; and whoever witnesses their savage grin of anger would not wish to approach to take a nearer view.' In George Scharf's lithograph two of the three bears can be seen. The Russian black bear in the pit was called Toby and was presented to the Society by the Marquis of Hertford who had previously kept him at his ancestral seat.

Camel House

This was built by Decimus Burton to house two Peruvian llamas but was later adapted for the camels. It can also be seen beyond the bear pit in the view on the *left*. The building still exists though so altered as to be almost unrecognisable.

Elephant Paddock

Jack, the Indian elephant, bought in 1831 at a cost of £420, was a great favourite. The woman who had been given permission to sell food for him, had, on one day, sold 36 shillings worth of cakes and buns 'all of which the elephant devoured'. Jack died in June 1847.

THE ROTUNDA, WOOLWICH

The Peace of 1814 was marked by the visit to London of the Allied Sovereigns to celebrate the abdication of Napoleon and rejoice, rather prematurely, in his overthrow. The Prince Regent went out of his way to entertain them and for their reception he had erected in the garden of Carlton House an enormous canvas tent designed by his favourite architect, John Nash.

It is this same tent which George Scharf painted in 1828 (*above*). Its removal to Woolwich is due to Colonel Sir William Congreve, a famous soldier and inventor of army rockets, who had succeeded his father as Superintendent of Military Machines at Woolwich and in this capacity was responsible for the collection of models and exhibits relating to the history of artillery which his father had begun. To house this collection Congreve persuaded the Prince Regent to give him the great tent when it was taken down from Carlton House garden. It was re-erected at Woolwich on 4 May 1820 and

Nash made it a permanent building by roofing it in lead and adding the central pillar to take extra weight.

This extraordinary building still stands today and although Nash's original canvas tent, which formed the museum's ceiling, was replaced by an exact replica in 1972, its present appearance is uncannily like Scharf's painting. It is not circular but twenty-four-sided, having a diameter of 116 ft and covering an area of 10,600 sq ft.

Some of the exhibits which Scharf saw are still there though the trophy of arms around the central pillar has been given to the Tower Armouries and the ship models have gone to the National Maritime Museum. Gone, too, are the models of harbours and fortifications which feature in Scharf's painting. The guide on the left is pointing to a round table on which is a diorama of St James's Park showing the original position of the Rotunda and behind that, sloping up high above the visitors, is a model of the Rock of Gibraltar.

7

THE CITY

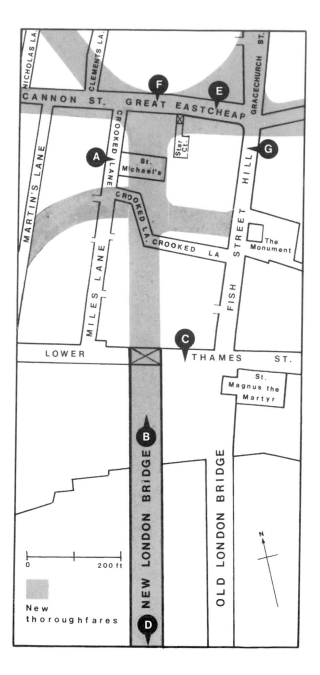

Map of the area around London Bridge showing the viewpoints from which George Scharf made his drawings

UNION ASSURANCE OFFICE
No 81 Cornhill on corner of Finch Lane

(*previous page*) Founded in 1714, its fire marks bearing the symbol of two pairs of clasped hands can still be seen on old houses.

CROOKED LANE

Crooked Lane runs straight south from Great Eastcheap on the left. Where it reaches the building being demolished it turns sharp left and soon bears right and left again; a truly crooked lane. The demolition is to make an opening for a new thoroughfare to lead to the Monument seen in the background. The other end of this thoroughfare can be seen on page 118.

Within a year, all the buildings seen here on the east side were to be pulled down to allow for the new approach road

to London Bridge. The greatest loss was the Wren church of St Michael. It remained in use until the demolition men were almost at its door. So close, indeed, that the last service held here on 20 March 1831 had to be abandoned. While the curate was reading the second lesson a piece of plaster fell and caused a slight disturbance, but it was assumed that some ruffian had thrown a piece of stone through the already broken west window and calmness was restored. However, when showers of plaster began to descend over the Com-munion table the crowded congregation made for the door. It was later discovered that there were no real grounds for alarm; the crumbling ceiling was due to workmen walking over the flat roof of the church to examine its condition. It was the poor children of the local charity schools who suffered most. There had been no time to take up the collection which was to have been devoted to their welfare.

Although a fragment of Crooked Lane existed until the 1950s all signs of it have now vanished.

NEW LONDON BRIDGE

As early as 1800 a committee had been set up to examine the possibility of rebuilding London Bridge which, after 600 years of use by traffic and abuse by the tidal buffeting of the Thames, had been declared unsafe. Architects were invited to submit plans but none of the suggestions was adopted and nothing more was done until 1822 when a prize was offered for the best design.

Although he was not among the first three winners, Sir John Rennie was awarded the contract by an over-riding committee of the House of Commons, and work began with the driving of the first pile for the first coffer-dam on 15 March 1824.

The City Corporation decided that such a momentous undertaking should not go unrecorded and, in 1830, they commissioned George Scharf to make some pictorial record of the building of the new bridge.

The watercolours which resulted were large and impressive. Two of them, each 5 ft long, depicted the construction of the approach roads on both sides of the river. They were destroyed in an air raid in 1941 but luckily Scharf had made lithographs of them. As the views were too large for single litho stones each was printed on two sheets joined together to make 5 ft long panoramas.

The one *above* shows the view looking northwards from the middle of the bridge's approach road as it cuts ruthlessly into the very heart of the City to continue as far as the Bank of England and become King William Street in honour of William IV who was to open the new bridge. It demolished 318 houses and carved through nine ancient thoroughfares. In the centre is the doomed church of St Michael, Crooked Lane, while on the right is St Magnus the Martyr standing at the head of old London Bridge with traffic still passing its door. Behind St Magnus, Thames Street runs under the approach road and continues out of the picture on the left.

The Old and New Bridge

This watercolour (*right*) was also done for the City Corporation but, unlike the view above, it was never made into a lithograph.

The viewpoint is looking south from the bottom of Fish Street Hill and shows a carriage emerging from the archway, still existing today, which carries the approach road over Thames Street. New London Bridge is already in use and the old bridge is in an advanced state of demolition.

113

LONDON BRIDGE: Southern Approach

This lithograph, made from the second of the two large water-colours which George Scharf painted for the City Corporation, shows the building of the southern end of London Bridge looking south.

It gives an invaluable view of Borough High Street, one of London's oldest thoroughfares. Since the earliest times it had been the approach road to London Bridge and was well supplied with inns which not only offered refreshment and accommodation for the traveller but served as depots for carrier wagons and passenger coaches to and from Kent, Surrey, Sussex and Hampshire.

The creation of the new bridge resulted in the total destruction of the western side of the High Street down to St Saviour's Church (since 1905, Southwark Cathedral) which was so dangerously close to the approach road that its beautiful thirteenth-century Lady Chapel was threatened. For two years antiquaries, supported by the Church, fought to save it. They finally won but a medieval extension known as Bishop Andrew's Chapel, seen above as the small buttressed building to the left of the Church, had to go.

On the eastern side of the High Street, the houses and shops which lined the roadway leading to Old London Bridge

(just out of the picture to the left) were also to be demolished within a year or two to create a large and beautiful open space with gardens surrounding the new northern extension of St Thomas's Hospital. All this was destroyed with the building of London Bridge station in 1843 and the formation of the Charing Cross railway extension in 1862 with its ugly viaduct crossing over Borough High Street just south of St Saviour's.

The first turning on the left is Tooley Street and the curious square building above it is a shot-tower used in the manufacture of gunshot. This was adapted as a semaphore signal station in 1842 but was burnt down in 1843.

Right By the time this drawing of the southern side of Tooley Street was made, the corner block which faced onto Borough High Street had been demolished as far back as Carter Lane, the turning on the right. The narrow lane between the warehouse and the old weather-boarded building is Joiners Street which opened into a small square and then continued southward almost as far as Guy's Hospital.

r of Gt Eastcheap and Fish Street Hill, City

June 1830

G. Scharf Del

E

GREAT EASTCHEAP

As can be seen on the map on p. 110, Great Eastcheap ran parallel to the River Thames and joined, at right angles, both the road to the old bridge, Fish Street Hill, and the road to the new bridge about to be built. In fact that was the extent of Great Eastcheap and Scharf's two pencil drawings show the whole of its south side, all about to be demolished to make way for the new London Bridge approaches. It continued on the west as Cannon Street and beyond Fish Street Hill it became Little Eastcheap.

The large building on the left (*above*) with the curved front-age is the same as that seen at the top of Fish Street Hill on p. 119, Evans' London Stove Grate Bazaar. It appears to be still open for business.

A narrow alley leads to Star Court, a tiny quadrangle flanked by three houses which backed on to the churchyard of St Michael's, Crooked Lane.

The second drawing (*above*) is a continuation of Great

Eastcheap westward which ends at the entrance to Crooked Lane. The house on the extreme right is in Cannon Street: No 49, the shop of John R. Morris, Cheesemonger.

On the other corner of Crooked Lane is the shop of Francis Willett, Gun Flint Manufacturer, the other side of which can be seen on p. 110.

Great Eastcheap was famous out of all proportion to its size solely because here was the site of one of the most renowned taverns in London's history: the Boar's Head. Traditionally the scene of Falstaff's roistering with Prince Hal in Shakespeare's *Henry IV*, it was first mentioned as early as the reign of Richard II. The original tavern was destroyed in the Great Fire but was rebuilt two years afterwards and its carved stone sign features prominently in Scharf's drawing. It is dated 1668 and bears the initials I.T. probably standing for John Thornicroft, a local ground landlord at this time. Happily the sign was rescued when the house was demolished

and can now be seen in the Museum of London.

The back windows of the tavern looked out upon the burial ground of St Michael's, Crooked Lane, and here was the tombstone of one Robert Preston 'late Drawer of the Boar's Head – who departed this Life March 16, Anno Domini 1730 aged 27 years'. The stone, with its long eulogistic inscription was saved and can now be seen at the church of St Magnus the Martyr. All the bodies from St Michael's churchyard were transferred to that of St Magnus at a cost of £2739 6s 11d.

The Boar's Head had ceased to be a tavern some time before 1790 and, when Scharf made his drawing, was divided into two tenements with shops occupied by a Tea Broker and a Wine Merchant.

The whole of this site was levelled and widened when King William Street was cut across it and it is today no more than a busy traffic junction where five roads meet.

FISH STREET HILL

Fish Street Hill slopes steeply down from Great Eastcheap to Old London Bridge which is to the left outside the picture.

For hundreds of years, ever since the thirteenth century when the bridge was built, all traffic crossing the river to enter or leave the City had trundled up or down this hill.

New London Bridge was built 180 ft upriver from the old bridge and Fish Street Hill, once one of the busiest thoroughfares in London, lost its importance. All the individual houses with their little shops on its western side, seen in this drawing, were demolished when the approach road to the new bridge was cut through their backyards.

Within seven years they were rebuilt as a unified terrace which included, in its centre, the Weigh House Chapel, belonging to a nonconformist congregation dating back to the seventeenth century whose old chapel had to be pulled down in the widening of the roads leading to the new bridge. The Chapel was opened in 1834 but demolished fifty years later to make way for one of the entrances to Monument Underground station.

The demolition on the left is to make an opening for a new thoroughfare called Arthur Street East, the present-day Monument Street, the other end of which can be seen on p. 111. Opposite the demolition and just out of the picture is the Monument itself casting its shadow across the foreground.

The turning on the right is Great Eastcheap leading to Cannon Street. Those evacuated shopkeepers who did not retire on their compensations set up shop elsewhere. The Toy Warehouse of Walton & Son next to the demolitions, whose house included the arched entrance to Bell Yard, moved to No 191 Bishopsgate Street Without. At No 5, Phillip & Daniel Green, Ironmongers, re-opened at No 124 Lower Thames Street.

Sir John Rennie, architect of New London Bridge, commissioned Scharf to make this drawing; it was later bought by John Edmund Gardner and is now in the Guildhall Collection of Prints and Drawings.

in Fleet Street, august 1830

FLEET STREET

This view (*above*) of Fleet Street looking west in August 1830 has changed out of all recognition and, as so often, Scharf has captured a scene just before the builders were due to arrive. About to be demolished is the ancient Church of St Dunstan-in-the-West sticking out 30 ft into the roadway with a shop built against its eastern wall. It was described by a contemporary who was not sorry to see it go as 'a medley of unredeemed ugliness – such a jumble of styles, or rather barbarous imitations of them – there is hardly anything so unique as was the rusticated piece of wall above some windows of carpenter's Gothic, and surmounted in its turn by battlements, above which, again, peeked a sort of capatious sentry-box [on the south side], containing the far-famed clock, with its two savages as big as life, who were wont to strike the chimes, to the great wonderment of gaping errand boys and country cousins, and to the no small profit of pick-

pockets and other cozeners.' The 'far-famed clock' can be seen projecting on its bracket from the south side of the church. It was made by Thomas Harris in 1671 and was an early clock in London to have a double face. In the alcove on the battlements is the stone statue of Queen Elizabeth I which dates from 1586 and originally stood on the west side of Ludgate. When the City gates were pulled down in 1760 the statue was given to Alderman Sir Francis Gosling who had it painted to resemble bronze and erected at St Dunstan-in-the-West two years later.

A month after this drawing was made, parts of the old church were put up for auction and the statue of Queen Elizabeth was sold for £16 10s. The clock, however, was not auctioned. The Marquis of Hertford, ever since seeing it as a small boy, had always wanted to possess it together with its bell-striking giants and now offered to buy it for 200 guineas. The St Dunstan's Vestry accepted the offer and the Marquis had the whole clock re-assembled at his villa in Regent's Park. One reason for demolishing the old church was to widen Fleet Street and the new church, as we can see today, was built 30 ft back in line with the shops. The first stone of the new St Dunstan's was laid in July 1831 and it was not until August 1832 that the east wall of the old church, which had been allowed to remain standing as a sort of screen, was removed to reveal the new church in all its glory. This was consecrated on 31 July 1833. The statue of Queen Elizabeth, lost sight of for some time, was eventually found in a cellar and in 1839 was put up over the vestry porch where it still stands. In 1935 Lord Rothermere bought the clock and returned it to St Dunstan's so that today the giants may still be seen striking their bells to the surprise of tourists and children.

In the distance Temple Bar, the barrier separating Westminster from the City of London, straddles the roadway at the west end of Fleet Street. Ever since the City gates had been pulled down there had been strong agitation for the same to happen to Temple Bar. It barely escaped when, at the end of the eighteenth century, Alderman Pickett, who added to the list of its obvious disadvantages the claim that it 'prevented the circulation of a free current of air', succeeded in carrying out his great Strand Improvement Scheme which widened that thoroughfare almost up to Temple Bar itself. But the City Corporation continually opposed its demolition. They could hardly deny that it was an impediment to traffic, and took advantage of it by demanding a toll of 2d from every non-freeman who drove his cart over the City boundary. But most of all it was the symbolic bar of their jurisdiction, the jealously held boundary over which even the Monarch had to seek permission to pass. So Temple Bar remained until 1878 when the City finally conceded the long battle. It was removed and re-erected at Theobald Park, Cheshunt, where it now languishes, the subject of a new controversy as to whether it should be returned to the City or not.

The Great Fire of 1666 just failed to reach three houses before St Dunstan's Church – the three seen in Scharf's drawing. The one adjacent to the church may have been rebuilt – it was certainly given a new stucco frontage in the eighteenth century – but there is no doubt about the Elizabethan orgin of its gabled and galleried neighbours. These houses were to survive until 1890.

CORNER OF BRIDE LANE

This was No 98 Fleet Street. Scharf's drawing (*above*) is not dated but the shop was occupied by Thomas Willows, Fishmonger, who was here in 1838, at which time No 99 next door was a public house called the Crown & Sugar Loaf. On 17 July 1841 the first number of *Punch* came out and a publican named Godwin P. Kennan joined the two premises together and called them Punch's Tavern & Restaurant. Though rebuilt, it bears the same name today but the story that *Punch* was actually conceived here has no basis in fact; the name of the pub was undoubtedly changed to cash in on the popularity of the new paper. In 1865 this corner building saw the early years of an organisation that was to become gigantic and famed throughout the world, for it was here that Thomas Cook & Son set up their first London office. A few years later they moved to the huge block directly opposite which they occupied until 1926.

Above   The Fleet Street end

Below   The Holborn Bridge end

FLEET MARKET

The Fleet River, rising in Hampstead and flowing into the Thames at Blackfriars, gave its name, not only to a universally known Street and a Prison made famous by Mr Pickwick, but also to a market which, because it had such a brief existence, is now almost forgotten. By the mid eighteenth century the Fleet River (or Ditch as it came to be known) was so notoriously filthy, little more than an open sewer, that it was covered over from Holborn Bridge to Fleet Street and the market built down the middle. The handsome market building, designed by George Dance the Elder, formed a piazza with a pretty clock tower in the middle. The whole market was 370 yds long with permanent shops for butchers, fishmongers, fruiterers, and dealers in herbs and roots. It even provided parking space for carts coming in from the country. It took over from the Stocks Market which was on the site of the Mansion House. For the stall-holders there was no break in trading. They were notified of the move on 5 August 1737; the old Stocks Market closed and the new Fleet Market opened on the following 30 September. Fleet Market lasted until 1829 when it was cleared away to make Farringdon Street and a replacement was built on its west side towards Shoe Lane. Called New Fleet Market when it was opened on 20 November 1829, it soon became known as Farringdon Market and stood until 1892.

Above   The Middle of the Market

Below   By the time Scharf saw the Market the year before it was demolished, some alterations had taken place, notably the erection in about 1800 of elegant little shops at each end. This is one of a pair at the Holborn Bridge or northern end.

SWEETINGS ALLEY

Sweetings Alley (*above*) was a narrow thoroughfare on the east side of the Royal Exchange. Though always busy as a short cut between Cornhill and Threadneedle Street, no one had ever depicted it before George Scharf made this drawing in about 1830. When he drew it he was standing with his back to the Royal Exchange looking east with Cornhill to his right and Threadneedle Street to his left. At the end of the passageway between the little lock-up shops is the New York Coffee House.

The original New York Coffee House was burnt down in 1759 together with several other premises so that what we see *above* probably dates from the re-building after that fire.

The shop on the left is that of Joseph Sykes, tobacconist, while on the right is the print shop of Samuel Knight, a name recollected by Thackeray in an article in the *Westminster Review* of June 1840: 'Knight's in Sweetings Alley; Fairburn's in a court off Ludgate Hill; Howe's in Fleet Street – bright enchanted palaces, which George Cruikshank used to people with grinning fantastical imps and merry harmless sprites – where are they? Fairburn's shop knows him no more; not only has Knight disappeared from Sweetings Alley, but, as we are given to understand, Sweetings Alley has disappeared from the face of the Globe.'

Soon after ten o'clock on the bitterly cold night of 10 January 1838 the north-west corner of the Royal Exchange was found to be on fire. Eight engines and sixty-three men were soon on the spot but because the fire plugs were frozen it was some time before they could get to work. The fire was able to get a hold and it spread disastrously, reaching the east side by 3.30 next morning, threatening the destruction of Sweetings Alley. As the *Gentleman's Magazine* reported in Feb. 1838: 'The inhabitants on both sides of this narrow court succeeded in removing the greatest portion of their furniture and stocks-in-trade, and, not withstanding the very small intervening space, the firemen, getting on to the roofs of the houses on the opposite side of the alley, directed a plentiful supply of water over the shops and houses below them, by which they were kept cool and preventing from igniting.'

In spite of their efforts, several buildings were burnt down and the only accident occurred when a wall on the corner of Sweetings Alley fell down, cutting a man's hand.

The houses which survived the fire were soon demolished to make way for the new Royal Exchange and the paved area behind it is approximately where Sweetings Alley once was.

portico erecting at the Middlesex Hospital 12 Septʳ 1840

8

BUILDING
GREAT & SMALL

CARLTON HOUSE TERRACE

When Carlton House was demolished in 1829, Nash designed two blocks of terrace houses to occupy the site. They took five years to erect and part of the façade facing St James's Park is here being built (*above*). The drawing shows the method of constructing the Corinthian columns, with an iron core surrounded by brick which is faced with stucco. The short Grecian Doric columns supporting the balustraded parapet are cast iron and only half-round as the one lying in the foreground clearly shows.

MARBLE ARCH

The drawing *below*, dated March 1830, shows Nash's new south-east wing of Buckingham Palace nearing completion. On the extreme right is a travelling crane busy with the erection of Marble Arch built originally as the grand entrance to the Palace before it was moved to its present site in 1851. The crane partly obscures the Arch a detail of which is seen above it.

Above 'Mr Yokney's (*sic*) house rebuilding. Corner of Bedford St. and Chandos St.' This corner house, which was No 10 Bedford Street, was built in the late eighteenth century and occupied in 1783 by Samuel Yockney, Grocer. After the 'modernisation' it continued as Yockney's until 1844 and was pulled down in 1910.

Below The building of a portico, typical of thousands still existing all over London. The technique, iron and brick finished in stucco, is exactly similar to that used at Carlton House Terrace.

Above 'A house, No 23, being altered in Francis Street, June 1834.' In fact it shows a private house being made into a shop. In the foreground is the wooden fascia board ready to be put into position.

Below 'The Public House corner of Francis Street and Alfred St. being improved Spring 1843.' Plasterers are at work: one appears to be casting and the other preparing to apply one of a pair of lion-headed consoles on the side of the doorway.

The View taken from the 9th Pillar on this side of the Quadrant

URLING'S

This rather grotesque composition (*left*) in a neo-Greek style is No 224 on the east side of Regent Street on the corner of Argyle Place.

When Scharf drew this detail of its shop front (*below*) in August 1826, George Frederick Urling had just moved in having transferred his lace business from No 147 Strand. Under royal patronage, since Queen Charlotte granted a warrant in 1817, his business was justifiably famous while his advertisements in ladies' journals were unusual for having actual samples of his lace inserted in them.

Regent Street
Oct. 1826

REGENT STREET

No London street is more aptly named. It was indeed the Prince Regent's street planned by his architect John Nash to link his existing palace of Carlton House with his intended villa in Regent's Park. By the time he ascended the throne as George IV he had lost interest in Carlton House and it was demolished; the villa in Regent's Park was never built. But Regent Street was and with it London was to experience a change more sudden and radical than anything it had ever seen before. Between 1818 and 1820 hundreds of poor houses in dozens of mean little streets were swept away, old scruffy thoroughfares on the planned route were quadrupled in width and everything rebuilt in dazzling stucco.

George Scharf's drawing (*above left*) gives some idea of the grand scale of Nash's wide triumphal way. Looking north, Vigo Street is on the left and the end of the Quadrant on the right. The Quadrant, a beautiful colonnade of Doric columns sweeping round in a great arc from the circus at Piccadilly, was designed to provide a covered walk for shoppers on a rainy day, but was demolished in 1848, condemned as a 'haunt for vice and immorality'.

The great change was as much social as architectural. In his written report which accompanied his plans, Nash made it clear that he intended his new street to form a physical barrier 'between the Streets and Squares occupied by the Nobility and Gentry' on the west, and the 'narrow Streets and meaner houses occupied by mechanics and the trading part of the community' on the east. He succeeded so effectually that even today, though his great street has been totally rebuilt, it still divides Soho from Mayfair as if a knife had cut them apart. The contrast is illustrated perfectly by the drawing *above*. It looks miles away from Regent Street but is in fact only a few yards from the east side. What appears to be a mere lean-to shed is actually No 17 Tyler Street, 'The Original Oyster Shop', where it joins King Street. Its extraordinary shallowness is explained by the fact that all the houses on the north side of Tyler Street followed a medieval building line which ran at an angle making them progressively shallower towards the King Street end. It is remarkable that today the building on this spot still has the same proportions. In 1882 Tyler Street became Foubert's Place and King Street was renamed Kingley Street.

LAST OF WESTMINSTER PALACE

One of Scharf's earliest drawings of London was the water-colour *above*, made in 1818, showing a part of the Old Palace of Westminster which survived the fire of 1834 but was demolished two years later. The view is looking east from New Palace Yard with a corner of Westminster Hall on the extreme right and a glimpse of the River Thames through the gap on the left. By the side of Westminster Hall are Exchequer buildings and the archway at the end leads to Speaker's Court. The chambers at right angles are all that remain of a much longer range of Elizabethan buildings which included an ancient water-gate leading down to the river. They were occupied at this time by various departments of the Exchequer but were once used for a far less prosaic purpose. The middle doorway, over which (though it does not appear in the drawing) was carved the date 1602 and the initials ER with a Tudor rose on a star, opened on to a stairway leading to the once infamous Star Chamber on the first floor.

At about 6.30 in the evening of 16 October 1834, the Houses of Parliament caught fire due to an overheated stove, and burnt throughout the night. Next morning George Scharf was there with his sketch-book before the ruins of the ancient buildings had stopped smouldering. Nearly every day for three weeks he was clambering over the roof of Westminster Hall, which had escaped the fire, making dozens of drawings from which he planned to make a huge panorama. The result of all this work is disappointing. All that remains are a few crude sketches and a very rough, 9 ft long watercolour in two parts, which is possibly a preliminary study for the finished painting which he intended to publish as a lithograph. The lithograph never materialised and the original painting, for which he received only £2.10s at auction just before his death,

now seems to be lost.

The two best drawings of the ruins appear here. They both show the burnt-out shell of St Stephen's Chapel, originally built in the fourteenth century as part of the Palace of Westminster but, at the time of the fire, used as the House of Commons. The view on the *left* shows the two side walls looking north. (Scharf has incorrectly noted 'looking East'.)

In the view *above* we are looking east towards the river, the side walls and east end of the Chapel still standing. On the left is the southern end of Westminster Hall and on the right is one of the original halls of Henry II's Palace which had been put to various uses over the centuries and was, at the time of the fire, the House of Lords. It is seen more clearly on p. 132.

G. Scharf sen.ʳ del

New and old Houses of Parliament in 1851.

HOUSES OF PARLIAMENT
IN TRANSITION

The fire of 1834 did not destroy the whole of Westminster Palace and the Houses of Parliament as can be seen in these drawings made in the 1850s. Although some post-fire building is evident in the drawing (*top left*), most of what can be seen was built before the fire. The most remarkable survival is the old House of Lords under which the fire actually started. This is the long building with the four semicircular windows. (The statue of Richard Coeur de Lion stands on the site today.) It was built in the reign of Henry II and was originally known as the Lesser or White Hall. It became the Court of Requests in which petitions of the King's subjects were heard, but in 1801 its interior was refurbished to become the House of Lords. After the fire it was taken over by the Commons who remained here until their new chamber was ready for them in 1852, and the Lords went to the Painted Chamber, another part of the old Palace which was only partially destroyed. The small low buildings on the left are made of timber and were erected as temporary accommodation for the various Parliamentary offices while the Houses of Parliament were being built.

Below left is a closer view of the buildings on the right of the preceding picture. The square towers surmounted by battlements were additions to the Old Palace made by Sir John Soane in the 1820s. The porch jutting out was the Royal Entrance which had become, since the fire, the entrance to the Lords. To the left is part of the Old House of Lords (at this time the Commons) with the semicircular windows, and in front of it are temporary buildings for Parliamentary officers. The four windows light the apartments of, from left to right, the Chaplain, the Serjeant-at-Arms, the Speaker's Secretary and the Speaker himself. The next, wooden, building with three windows is the South Lobby of the House of Commons.

The drawing below shows the state of progress of the Houses of Parliament by 1851. Barry's familiar Tudor skyline has already taken shape while the half-completed Victoria Tower is immediately recognisable. The New Houses of Parliament extended much farther south than the old buildings and a number of Georgian houses on the east side of Abingdon Street were demolished in the process. One of them still stands to the left of the Victoria Tower. On the extreme right Abingdon Street now begins at No 11, Chequers Inn.

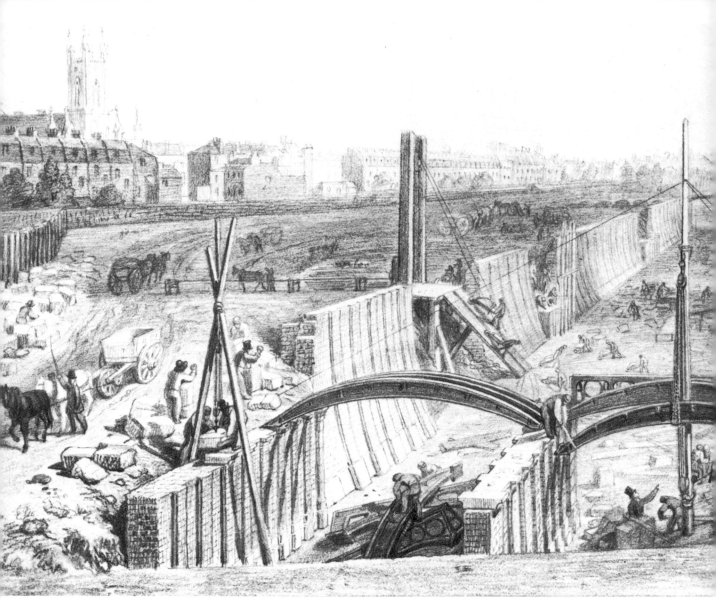

The Birmingham Railway
constructing near Regent
Park, April 1836
J Scharf del

BUILDING THE BIRMINGHAM RAILWAY

London's second railway, the London to Birmingham, was authorised by Act of Parliament on 6 May 1833 and originally came no closer into London than Chalk Farm in Camden Town just north of the Regent's Canal. Work began on the terminus there in 1834 but in the following year another Act was obtained allowing the line to go forward another $1\frac{1}{4}$ miles to Euston. It is this Euston Extension Line which is being constructed in Scharf's drawing *above* dated May 1836. Work is well in advance since the line was opened less than a year later on 20 July 1837. The view is looking south towards Euston at the spot where the line goes under the Hampstead Road. The extension caused difficult engineering problems. Chalk Farm being so much higher than Euston and the necessity to carry the line over the Regent's Canal combined

to create a considerable gradient down to the terminus. This gradient, as steep as 1 in 70 in places, was too severe for the light steam locomotives then in use and the trains were hauled up to Camden by cable. Coming in from the north, engines were uncoupled at Camden and the carriages released to coast down the incline on their own volition controlled by a brakeman. This extraordinary system lasted only seven years but for some time later trains were helped up the incline with an extra engine pushing from behind.

The drawing on the *left* shows the method used to haul barrows up and down an incline by attaching them to an 'endless' chain pulled by a horse.

ROYAL COLLEGE OF SURGEONS

In 1800 the Royal College of Surgeons moved from their premises in the Old Bailey to a house on the south side of Lincoln's Inn Fields, No 41. When they acquired the great anatomical collection formed by John Hunter, they found that they had no room to accommodate it and in 1803 they purchased the adjoining house, No 42. George Dance, the younger, was commissioned to design a new building on the sites of Nos 41 and 42 and it was opened in 1813. The building was quite unpretentious but it did have a fine portico with six unfluted Ionic columns. With additions to the museum and the rapidly increasing library, more expansion became necessary and in 1834, with the acquisition of No 40 on the east side, a complete re-building was undertaken with Sir Charles Barry as the architect. Barry wanted to do away with the old portico which now, because of the extension of the site eastward, would no longer be centrally placed. He was not allowed to do so, however, and had to overcome the problem by removing one column from the western end of the portico and re-erecting it on the eastern end.

Right　In October 1834 this view, taken from the south-east, shows five of the portico's six columns still standing. The sixth column at the western end has been carefully taken down and was later re-assembled at the eastern end.

Below　By July 1834, No 40 Lincoln's Inn Fields, on the east side of the College of Surgeons, had already gone and the wall behind the College's portico was being demolished. On the skyline can be seen the roof lanterns of the old museum.

g. Scharf del July 1834

ROYAL COLLEGE OF SURGEONS
Museum Girders

The new museum to house the Hunterian Collection which Sir Charles Barry designed for the Royal College of Surgeons was 91 ft long, 39 ft wide and 35 ft high. The iron girders used in the skylighted roof were cast at Joseph Bramah's Foundery in Pimlico and, being too large for any wagon, an ingenious method of conveyance was devised (*above*) which consisted in merely attaching wheels to them.

Below Each girder, over 39 ft long and representing the span of the museum roof, carried its own tackle which was assembled upon arrival to support the girder while its wheels were removed. It was then manhandled on to the site on rollers ready for hoisting into position in the roof.

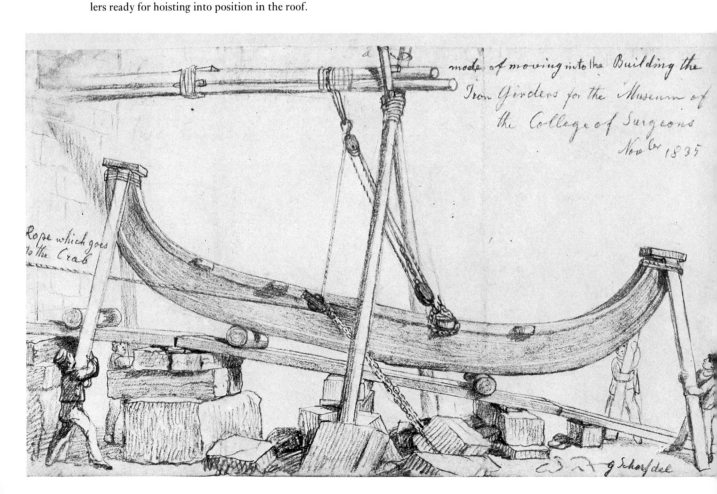

A. Tottenham

9

RURAL LONDON

TOTTENHAM

In the 1820s when George Scharf was making these drawings, Tottenham was a quiet village set in a rural landscape dotted around with great houses erected by aristocrats and retired merchants. It also had its share of pretty cottages such as the one on p. 139 and country retreats for businessmen who worked in the City. The painting (*upper left*) is of West Green, Tottenham, then a triangular meeting of roads with a pond in the middle about half a mile west of the main highway. The house with its distinctive dove-cote has never been identified.

Above This view is just off Tottenham High Road looking

east along Baily's Lane towards the River Lee. Today it is Craven Park Road. In this house, in 1751, was born Priscilla Wakefield, the Quaker philanthropist and writer of children's books.

Below left 'Rev Dr Schwabe's House.' This was a boys' boarding school on the west side of the High Road opposite Baily's Lane set back from the road behind its trim lawn.

Below Typical of the area's more humble dwellings is this terrace called Sidney Place. It was on the east side of Stamford Hill just as it became Stoke Newington High Street.

At Hampstead
G. S... near L..

ISLINGTON

This (*below*) is George Scharf's first London drawing. It is dated 1816 when it was still the 'merrie Islington' of open fields, a place where Londoners took summer evening strolls, where they could still, as in the days of Stow, 'refresh their dulled spirits in the sweet and wholesome air'. The view is looking south with the tower of St Mary's Church in the centre and the dome of St Paul's Cathedral in the distance on the left. Winding across the picture is the New River, the artificial channel cut by Sir Hugh Myddleton in the seventeenth century to bring fresh water to London from Amwell in Hertfordshire.

JACK STRAW'S CASTLE, HAMPSTEAD

The name, over which historians have argued for years, is probably nothing more than a generic term for a rustic as Jack Tar is for a sailor, while equally obscure is the origin of the inn itself though it is known, from documentary evidence, to have existed in 1714.

Scharf's drawing (*left*), made in 1830, shows a plain stucco façade with Regency bow windows fronting a much older building. This is how it must have looked when Charles Dickens first showed it to his friend John Forster. Dickens, busy writing *Pickwick Papers* at the time, needed relaxation and had sent a note to Forster which read: '"You don't feel disposed, do you, to muffle yourself up, and start off with me for a good brisk walk over Hampstead Heath? I knows a good 'ous there where we can have a red-hot chop for dinner, and a glass of good wine." – 'which led', wrote Forster, 'to our first experience of Jack Straw's Castle, memorable for many happy meetings in coming years.'

By about 1840 a hotel called the Castle was added to the side of the inn replacing the small weather-vaned building on the left. The inn was badly damaged in the Second World War and rebuilt in 1961. The railings on the right surround Heath House still standing at the angle between New End Way and Spaniards Road.

In Jack Straw's tea-garden (*below*) the weather-boarding behind the inn reveals its antiquity. The man in the foreground appears to be lighting his pipe from a gas-jet fixed to a tree, though how it works is not clear, while in the background a steaming copper supplies hot water for tea.

'SOUTH ROW, OLD BROMPTON'
(Above)

This is now called Hogarth Place just off the east side of Earl's Court Road opposite the Underground station. The view, lit by the early morning sun, is looking north-east and shows the back of the White Hart Tavern which dated from at least 1722 and was not demolished until 1869.

'LOWER ROAD, BROMPTON', 1822
(Below)

No other views of this building exist, and there was no Lower Road, Brompton. Presumably Scharf meant Lower Grove, one of the names given to part of Brompton Road above today's Ovington Square. Here was a handsome detached mansion called Grove House and it is probable that this long castellated building could have been the riding school attached to it or even the drawing-room which was added for the entertainment of the Prince Regent.

'BROMPTON', 1822 *(Above)*

This is today's Fulham Road looking east from near the top of Pond Place. At one time the houses on the right backed on to Chelsea Common, a tract of open land extending down to King's Road where cattle grazed. After 1790 it began to be built on and although by Scharf's time it was dotted with small houses, the large pond which provided the cattle with water was still very much in evidence. If the passengers in the coach looked to their right they would see it through the gap in the houses they were about to pass. It was an attractive

spot which must have drawn many a Londoner on a pleasant summer's evening for here was the Stag Tavern pleasure garden complete with bowling green beside the pond. On the left a man is sitting on a stile at the entrance to a footpath which goes up to Old Brompton. It ran along the west side of Harrison & Bristow's Nursery which covered 27 acres. There had been nursery grounds at Brompton since the end of the seventeenth century and by the 1820s the area was still mainly horticultural with just a scattering of cottages and small houses among the market gardens. The gradual increase of building development as the roads got nearer to central London is perfectly demonstrated in Scharf's drawing where long terraces begin to appear as the distant road approaches Knightsbridge. Harrison & Bristow's Nursery still opens up the land on the left but ten years after this drawing was made the nurserymen went bankrupt and Pelham Crescent was built on this site.

WOOLWICH

George Scharf had served in the Royal Engineers at Waterloo and it is more than likely that he lived for a time in Woolwich with friends he had made in the army. Certainly the great number of drawings he did of Woolwich suggest more than just a visit. The most detailed is this panorama (*above*) which he drew in 1825 looking north across the Thames from the high ground in the vicinity of today's Hillreach. On the right is the tower of St Mary's Church, which is still standing, but the houses in the foreground have yet to be identified. The building prominent in the centre of the left half presents a fascinating enigma. Just about on this site there was a pub called the Edinburgh Castle which we know, from other drawings, looked quite like the house in the panorama. However, George Scharf's wife Elizabeth made a pencil sketch of what is unquestionably this same building on which George has written, 'not the Edinburg (*sic*) Castle.' William Thomas Vincent, the Woolwich historian, gave an address to the local antiquarian society in 1908 on some of Scharf's drawings and suggested that the inn which Elizabeth drew was the Salutation. But the Salutation was near the Ropeyard, east of St Mary's Church and well out of the panorama on the right. The identity of the inn remains a mystery.

Unity Place *(Below)*

This was a row of houses on the west side of Samuel Street where Vincent suggested Scharf may have lodged. They were only recently demolished.

Bowater Cresent *(Right)*

A continuation of Samuel Street, the houses here furnished lodgings for officers who did not chose to live in the Barracks opposite.

OLD KENT ROAD

Though one of the main roads out of London – the Canterbury and Dover Road – it had no great coaching inns. It did, however, have several ale-houses and some sixteen taverns which enjoyed a local trade and catered for the drovers and farmers who brought their produce into London from Kent. Typical of these humble taverns was the Castle painted by Scharf in 1827. It stood on the east side a little south of the much more famous World Turned Upsidedown.

Today the Castle is still there though rebuilt. It stands between Hendre Road and Marcia Road.

Sources of Illustrations

Each item in the British Museum Department of Prints and Drawings which is mounted in the Folios is given its *Book* number, *Page* number and *Individual* number in brackets, followed by its measurements in millimetres with the vertical dimension preceding the horizontal. Items kept in Solander Boxes are given their *Box* number, *Register* number and *Individual* number in brackets followed by dimensions. The dimensions are for the area of the paper on which the drawing was made. 'Detail' after the dimensions implies that only one of a number of drawings on the same sheet has been reproduced or that only part of a drawing has been used.

Title Page Tottenham BM Box 17a 1862–6–14 (142) 234 × 326

*p.*5 National Portrait Gallery, London

6/7 Author's Collection

8 *Top* BM Book 6 p. 19 (71) 285 × 203

8 *Bottom* BM Box 17c 1862–6–14 (80) 240 × 376

9 Author's Collection

10 Author's Collection

12 Guildhall, London

13 Zoological Society, London

16 *Top* BM Book 4 p. 16 (647) 268 × 404

16 *Bottom* BM Book 4 p. 14 (645) 303 × 463

19 BM Book 6 p. 56 (102) 225 × 132

20 BM Book 4 p. 4 (8) 226 × 324 Detail

21 *Top* BM Book 4 p. 2 (5) 172 × 297 (an identical drawing is in the Westminster Local Col.)

21 *Bottom* BM Book 6 p. 53 (105) 222 × 180

22 *Top* BM Book 6 p. 60 (10) 230 × 415

22 *Bottom* BM Box 17c 1862–6–14 (118) 140 × 230

23 BM Book 6 p. 51 (96) 455 × 730

24 *Top* Greater London Record Office & Historical Library

24 *Bottom* BM Box 17c 1862–6–14 (121) 227 × 134

25 *Top* BM Book 6 p. 52 (97) 140 × 400

25 *Bottom* BM Book 4 p. 5 (100) 227 × 217

26 BM Book 6 p. 55 (110) 165 × 275

27 BM Book 6 p. 53 (106) 261 × 177

29 *Top* BM Book 4 p. 3 (7) 139 × 305

29 *Bottom* BM Book 6 p. 52 (99) 135 × 350

30 *Below left* BM Box 17c 1862–6–14 (107) 256 × 173

31 *Top* BM Book 6 p. 55 (11) 139 × 225 and (109) 133 × 226

31 *Centre* Author's Collection (identical drawing BM Book 6 p. 56 (108))

32 BM Box 17c 1862–6–14 (119) 138 × 228

33 Guildhall. Detail from sheet of pen drawings

34 *Top* BM Box 17b 1862–6–14 (1187) 136 × 221

35 *Top* BM Box 17b 1862–6–14 (1188) 134 × 219

35 *Bottom* BM Box 17a 1862–6–14 (1192) 140 × 230

36 *Top* BM Book 1 p. 2 (807) 102 × 228

36 *Bottom* BM Book 1 p. 4 (1147) 135 × 140

37 *Top* BM Book 1 p. 2 (1189) 139 × 90

37 *Bottom* BM Book 1 p. 3 (1090) 140 × 230

38 *Top* BM Book 1 p. 3 (1136) 125 × 227

38 *Bottom* BM Book 2 p. 23 (1085) 126 × 124

39 *Top* BM Book 2 p. 22 (1087) 137 × 230

39 *Bottom* BM Book 2 p. 23 (1176) 200 × 137 Detail

40 Both on same sheet. BM Book 2 p. 21 (813) 203 × 142

41 BM Book 2 p. 21 (814) 187 × 135

42 *Top* BM Book 2 p. 21 (1141) 159 × 127

42 *Bottom* BM Book 2 p. 21 (1138) 80 × 80

43 *Top* BM Book 2 p. 21 (1140) 120 × 110

43 *Bottom* BM Book 2 p. 14 (962) 128 × 207 Detail

44 BM Box 17c 1862–6–14 (122) 219 × 122

45 BM Box 17c 1862–6–14 (120) 132 × 175

46 BM Box 17d 1900–7–25 (17) 110 × 189 Detail

47 *Top* BM Book 2 p. 24 (1120) 139 × 164

47 *Bottom* BM Book 2 p. 24 (1122) 228 × 138

48 *Top* BM Book 2 p. 10 (910) 193 × 127 Detail

48 *Bottom* & 49 BM Book 2 p. 10 (351) 142 × 225

50 BM Book 2 p. 5 (1004) 226 × 140

51 *Top* BM Book 2 p. 6 (905) 70 × 130

51 *Bottom* BM Book 2 p. 6 (903) 75 × 70

52 BM Book 2 p. 7 (1012–1015) 225 × 140

53 *Both* BM Book 2 p. 7 (19) 110 × 227

54 *Top* BM Box 17b 1862–6–14 (976) 130 × 140

54 *Bottom left* BM Box 17b 1862–6–14 (940) 137 × 235 Detail

54 *Bottom right* BM Book 2 p. 14 (962) 128 × 207 Detail

55 *Top left* BM Box 17a 1900–7–25 (45) 113 × 70

55 *Top right* BM Book 2 p. 15 (979) 127 × 175 Detail

55 *Bottom* BM Box 17b 1862–6–14 (988) 230 × 136 Detail

56 *Top* BM Box 17b 1862–6–14 (988) 230 × 136 Detail

56 *Centre* BM Book 2 p. 18 (932 & 933) 227 × 130 Detail

56 *Bottom* BM Box 17b 1862–6–14 (986) 235 × 132 Detail

57 BM Book 4 p. 3 (9) 180 × 252 Detail

58 *Bottom* BM Book 6 p. 28 (32) 140 × 222

59 *Top* BM Book 6 p. 27 (23) 340 × 475

59 *Bottom* BM Book 6 p. 28 (56) 226 × 200

60 BM Book 4 p. 7 (18) 210 × 240

61 *Top left* BM Book 4 p. 7 (14) 220 × 124

61 *Top right* BM Book 4 p. 5 (13) 226 × 140

61 *Bottom* BM Book 4 p. 43 (77) 222 × 140

62 *Top* BM Book 4 p. 1 (12) 220 × 590

62 *Bottom* BM Book 4 p. 38 (92) 140 × 228

63 *Top right & bottom* BM Book 2 p. 48 (1042) 152 × 139

64 BM Box 17c 1862–6–14 (20) 198 × 453

65 *Bottom* BM Box 17c 1862–6–14 (19) 217 × 371 Detail

66 BM Book 4 p. 1 (2) 225 × 280

67 *Left* BM Book 4 p. 36 (90) 230 × 136

67 *Top right* BM Book 4 p. 40 (93) 221 × 136

67 *Bottom right* BM Book 4 p. 37 (56) 96 × 138 Detail

68 BM Book 4 p. 40 (76) 138 × 227

69 BM Book 1 p. 12 (1131) 153 × 140 Detail

Location of George Scharf's Work

BRITISH MUSEUM: Department of Prints & Drawings

The bulk of Scharf's work is located in this department catalogued under 'Foreigners working in England: Period III'. It ranges from highly finished watercolours to slight pencil sketches and is contained in six large volumes, five solander boxes, two sketch-books and some portfolios. Their contents are summarised here; a photocopy of the author's detailed catalogue describing each drawing can be consulted in the department.

Book vol. 1 Pages 1–4 advertising; 5–6 beggars; 7–20 building operations (11–12 paving; 12–16 sewers, gas and waterpipes; 18–20 Birmingham Railway); 21 country characters; 22–5 election scenes; 26–31 furniture, ironmongery; 32–41 London types; 42–4 Lord Mayors' Shows; 45 military uniforms; 46–8 musicians; 49–50 oriental types; 51–2 schools; 53–4 shipping; 55–9 liveries.

vol. 2 1–10 street vendors; 11–23 street musicians and entertainers; 22–3 Vauxhall Gardens and fairs; 24–32 trades and occupations; 33–54 vehicles and methods of transport; 55–6 coffee houses; 57–9 interiors; 60–2 kitchens; 61 hospitals; 62v public houses.

vol. 3 Pages 1–15 British Museum; 16–18 Old Bailey & Newgate; 19–20 Zoo; 20 Vauxhall Gardens; 21–3 Adelaide Gallery & Polytechnic; 24–7 Guildhall; 28–46 Houses of Parliament & Westminster Hall; 47 coroner's inquest; 48–9 lectures; 50–2 art exhibitions.

vol. 4 Pages 1–8 Strand, Charing Cross, St Martin's Lane; 9 Suffolk Street, Cockspur Street; 10–11 London Bridge; 12 Thames Tunnel & Vauxhall Bridge; 13–17 Torrington Square; 18–24 Tottenham Court Road & neighbourhood; 25 Tower of London; 26–8 University College Hospital & School; 29–43 shops.

vol. 5 Pages 1–2 Brompton, Hammersmith; 3 Clapham, Dulwich; 4 Clapton; 5 Edmonton; 6 Eltham; 7 Hampstead, Highgate; 8 Kew Gardens; 9 Lewisham, Wandsworth; 10 Mitcham; 11 Shooters Hill; 12–15 Stamford Hill; 16–17 Stoke Newington, Islington, Kingsland; 18–29 Tottenham; 20 Wimbledon, Richmond; 23–32 Woolwich.

vol. 6 Pages 1 Aldersgate, Bishopsgate; 2–3 Bank, Mansion House; 4 Blackfriars Bridge; 5 Bloomsbury; 6–7 Cannon Street, Gracechurch Street, St Paul's; 8 Royal College of Surgeons; 9–11 Crooked Lane; 12 Cornhill, Newgate Street; 13 East India Docks, Brunswick Theatre; 14 Euston station; 15 Fish Street Hill; 16–25 Francis Street; 26 Gray's Inn Lane; 27–8 Hungerford Market; 29 Hyde Park; 30 Lambeth, Camden Road; 31–5 London Bridge, St Olave; 36 Ludgate, St Martin; 37 Ludgate Hill; 38 Oxford Street, Savile Row; 39 Regent's Park; 40 Regent Street; 41–2 Southwark; 43 St Bartholomew's Hospital; 44–5 St James's Park; 46–59 St Martin's Lane, Covent Garden; 60–1 Strand.

Solander Box 17A Woolwich; soldiers; children; advertising men; posters; Finsbury; Tottenham; Brompton.

Solander Box 17B Old British Museum; coffee houses; advertising men; Gurney's steam carriage stage coach; men going to work; street musicians; street hawkers; Westminster Abbey.

Solander Box 17C Regent Street Quadrant; Golden Lane; St Martin's Lane; Bishopsgate Street; Strand; Charing Cross; Woolwich; Francis Street; Holloway; St Pancras; Covent Garden Market; Hampstead; Brookes's Museum, Blenheim Street.

Solander Box 17D Islington; paviors; election celebration; milk sellers; Stamford Hill; Dorking; Tottenham; water mains; Norwood.

Solander Box 17E Contains no London material. (Contents include several portraits and a Panorama of Donaustauf.)

Solander Box (Imperial) vol. 2 British Museum; smithy in Woolwich Dockyard; St Stephen's Chapel, Westminster.

Atlas Case 18 St Stephen's Chapel after the fire; Panorama of Thames from St Saviour's, Southwark; entrance hall of Royal Academy, Somerset House.

Sketchbook 198A24 Scenes and figures in London streets; St James's Park, Kensington; Vauxhall; Tottenham; Dulwich; Stamford Hill.

Sketchbook 198A25 Scenes and figures in London streets.

BRITISH LIBRARY: Department of Manuscripts

The department holds Scharf's German drawings and panoramas. The London material is contained in volume Add. 36489A. Summarised as follows: Nos 13–20 Greenwich; 21–2 Lee and Plumstead; 23–38 Woolwich; 40–53 The City including London Bridge; 69 King's Mews; 71 Vauxhall; 80 Regent Street; 85 Knightsbridge; 88 Bloomsbury Square; 99 Highgate Hill; 103 Wandsworth; 108 Bermondsey.

Details of all the London drawings in this volume are included in the Scharf catalogue in the Department of Prints & Drawings.

GUILDHALL LIBRARY

Old and New London Bridge from the south side of the Thames; Old and New London Bridge from Fish Street Hill; Crooked Lane; Fish Street Hill; Lord Mayor's Banquet; Castle Tavern, Old Kent Road; Procession of Society of Brass Founders and Braziers; sheet of characters.

VICTORIA & ALBERT MUSEUM

Interior of the Gallery of the New Society of Painters in Water Colours; Mitcham Common.

HOLBORN CENTRAL LIBRARY

Gray's Inn Lane (identical with BM Book 6 p. 26 (86)).

WESTMINSTER LIBRARY Local Collection

Charing Cross; King's Mews.

MUSEUM OF LONDON

Royal Academy, Somerset House.

ROYAL COLLEGE OF SURGEONS

Six highly finished watercolours showing rebuilding and roof views.

YALE CENTER FOR BRITISH ART (USA)

Swan Stairs, London Bridge; St Paul's, Deptford; Reigate Heath.

GREATER LONDON RECORD OFFICE & HISTORY LIBRARY

Some interesting drawings by George Scharf jun. when he was a boy.

HARINGEY LIBRARY, BRUCE CASTLE

An oil painting of Hornsey High Street.

Index